# CLARK GABLE

*The Pictorial Treasury of Film Stars*

# CLARK GABLE

## by
## RENE JORDAN

*General Editor:* **TED SENNETT**

GALAHAD BOOKS • NEW YORK CITY

To my mother,
a Gable fan

This Galahad Books edition is published by
arrangement with Pyramid Communications, Inc.

Copyright © 1973 by Pyramid Communications, Inc.

ISBN 0-88365-160-2

Library of Congress Catalog Card Number: 73-90212

Printed in the United States of America

# PREFACE

By TED SENNETT

"The movies!" Flickering lights in the darkness that stirred our imaginations and haunted our dreams. All of us cherish memories of "going to the movies" to gasp at feats of derring-do, to roar with laughter at clownish antics, to weep at acts of noble sacrifice. For many filmgoers, the events on the screen were not only larger than life but also more mysterious, more fascinating, and—when times were bad—more rewarding. And if audiences could be blamed for preferring movies to life, they never seemed to notice, or care.

Of course the movies have always been more than a source of wish-fulfillment or a repository for nostalgic memories. From the first unsteady images to today's most experimental efforts, motion pictures have mirrored America's social history, and over the decades they have developed into an internationally esteemed art.

As social history, movies reflect our changing tastes, styles, and ideas. To our amusement, they show us how we looked and behaved: flappers with bobbed hair and bee-stung lips cavorting at "wild" parties; gangsters and G-men in striped suits and wide-brimmed hats exchanging gunfire in city streets; pompadoured "swing-shift" Susies and dashing servicemen, "working for Uncle Sam." To our chagrin, they show us the innocent (and sometimes not so innocent) lies we believed: that love triumphs over all adversity and even comes to broad-shouldered lady executives; that war is an heroic and virtually bloodless activity; that fame and success can be achieved indiscriminately by chorus girls, scientists, football players, and artists. To our edification, they show us how we felt about marriage in the twenties, crime in the thirties, war in the forties, big business in the fifties, and youth in the sixties. (Presumably future filmgoers will know how we felt about sex in the seventies.)

As an influential art, motion pictures are being studied and analyzed as never before by young filmgoers who are excited by the medium's past accomplishments and its even greater potential for the future. The rich body of films from *Intolerance* to *The Godfather;* the work of directors from Griffith to Kubrick; the uses of film for documenting events, ideas, and even emotions—these are the abundant materials from which film courses and film societies are being created across the country.

THE PICTORIAL TREASURY OF FILM STARS also draws on these materials, encompassing in a series of publications all the people, the trends, and the concepts that have contributed to motion pictures as nostalgia, as social history, and as art. The books in the series range as widely as the camera-eye can take us, from the distant past when artists with a vision of film's possibilities shaped a new form of expression, to the immediate future, when the medium may well undergo changes as innovative as the first primitive movements.

THE PICTORIAL TREASURY OF FILM STARS is a tribute to achievement: to the charismatic stars who linger in all our memories, and to the gifted people behind the cameras: the directors, the producers, the writers, the editors, the cameramen. It is also a salute to everyone who loves movies, forgives their failures, and acknowledges their shortcomings, who attends Bogart and Marx Brothers revivals and Ingmar Bergman retrospectives and festivals of forthcoming American and European films.

"The movies!" The cameras turn and the flickering images begin. And again we settle back to watch the screen, hoping to see a dream made real, an idea made palpable, or a promise fulfilled. On that unquenchable hope alone, the movies will endure.

# CONTENTS

# ACKNOWLEDGMENTS

For help in obtaining photographs, I should like to thank William Pratt, Jerry Vermilye, Kenneth G. Lawrence, and *Movie Star News*. I should also like to thank Douglas Lemza of *Films Incorporated* for permitting me to screen Gable films.

Before Gable and after Gable: these are the two basic periods in the history of the male image on American screens. He was the watershed, the dividing line signaling the end of an era and the beginning of another. If Gable had not existed, Hollywood would have invented him.

He was as inevitable as the coming of sound. When Al Jolson in *The Jazz Singer* said "You ain't heard nothin' yet," not one of the pre-Vitaphone romantic idols would have been capable of mouthing that line without getting an involuntary laugh. Valentino, Novarro, or Gilbert would have brought the house down.

Those men thrived on silence, for silence is the realm of dreams. Waking up in the morning, we usually remember what we *did* in dreams, seldom if ever what we *said*. Silent films were dreamlike pantomimes and the stars communicated with a rapt audience through title cards, a sign language not meant for the human voice and as deceptive as the subtitles that mask the unreality of many foreign films now taken at face value.

Gable and the talkies did not bring reality into thirties films. They ushered in a different kind of unreality. Those were hard times and Depression-bound au-

# THE RIGHT TIME FOR THE RIGHT FACE

diences were not in the mood for Ruritanian kingdoms and imperious sheiks. A tough, anti-aristocratic feeling was in the air. Men had always been slightly wary of the effete silent heart-throbs, but now even women began to secretly turn against them.

Under these strained circumstances, it became increasingly foolish to envy or covet Prince Charming in a hussar's uniform. Then, suddenly, there was Gable to democratize the longings of the masses. As he portrayed them, the new brand of somewhat shopworn illusions were equally unattainable but they were not entirely idiotic. The Gable fantasies did not involve fancy dress and childish aspirations. They offered at least a low level of sanity anyone could hang onto in a paranoid world.

The movies desperately needed someone like Gable and he was in the right place at the right time with the right face. Ears too big, manners too rough, he emerged as the populist thirties Everyman. Men could identify with him as he went about

9

*CLARK GABLE. An early portrait*

10

dispensing vicarious thrills such as telling the boss where to get off or bringing the haughty heiress down a peg. For women, he was a promise of powerful, earthy sexuality that could hopefully be found at the Woolworth counter. Social tremors had shaken them from their dreams of marrying oriental potentates, so it was consoling to find a "regular guy" who could be so roughly sweet to fallen women and working girls, as well as disrespectful to highfalutin' ladies.

Gable was the NRA, bargain basement concept of sex and defiance for the otherwise deprived. An ideal mirror for harassed clerks and henpecked husbands, he adopted a leering attitude of withering disdain toward anything that was "uppity." Years before, Chaplin's uncanny sense of social comedy had been based on giving the pratfall to the bespatted capitalist, never the beggar. Gable filtered the technique into sexual mores and in his best debunking of elegant ladies he was like a straight-faced version of Groucho Marx's atrocious treatment of the lofty Margaret Dumont.

Gable's ruthless realism made him the first great antihero of American movies, a Don Quixote in reverse, who saw the windmill in every giant and the whore in every lady. Before a generation coined the term, he invented *cool.* He was able to wade through the worst of MGM's syrupy sentimentality and shake it off, without a single ruffle to his feathers.

Thirties stars often had a third person attitude about their screen images. Before tackling a part, Tracy said he always asked himself what Tracy would do as a judge or a lawyer. There are tales about Garbo watching her old films and gasping nervously: "Oh, look what she's going to do now. Ah, she is shameless."

Gable's reaction was similar, except that in his case it was probably unconscious and therefore more spontaneous and charming to watch. He would have been highly suspicious of anyone who called him a Brechtian actor, yet he unknowingly was one. His detachment was miles away from the Stanislavskian school of acting by identification, brought to films by Brando, Steiger, and the Actor's Studio crowd. Gable did not "live" the part, but often merely showed it, held it before the audience by keeping himself one or two steps removed.

Frequently involved in melodramas he personally considered ludicrous, he was the least de-

11

luded among his contemporaries. Garbo was titillated by the films she was in; Crawford believed in them implicitly; Tracy did not, but he lacked the impudence to let it show. Only Gable had the cheek (dimpled) to let the audience in on the game. He let the men know that he wasn't hoodwinked by the heroine's pretensions. He let the women know that those puritanical plots might defang but never castrate the randy tomcat he played.

Gable was at his best in comedy, where he could laugh with ease at the madness around him. Still, he was able to weave his way into the fabric of the worst melodramatic plot and play it on three levels, so that those who came to cry got their quota of tears, while the cynics who came to sneer did not hold the "sob-stuff" too much against him. The third level is surely unconscious and his demi-smirks in films like *Chained* and *Susan Lenox* are like secret coded messages, conveying to those who would watch his films in the future that he stood away from the nonsense and was keeping his cool.

Cool, of course, is a weapon as well as a shield, and it let Gable get away with outrageous behavior. In *Too Hot to Handle* he was a newsreel cameraman unable to get actual shots of the Sino-Japanese war and enterprisingly faking them with a screaming half-naked baby and a toy airplane. It is the kind of cheap exploitation of suffering that would have made anyone else repulsive, but Gable could do it and still remain a rascally hero, because the audience is in on the joke, even thirty years later.

By sheer sleight-of-hand, he was able to remove the moral issue from nearly all he did on the screen. He was the fast talker, the operator, sometimes the con man, two steps ahead of the law, cynical child of a cynical age. For the Gable thirties man, not having money was the one unforgivable sin and he was capable of procuring it in ways that were often shady and morally unacceptable. The audience admired him nonetheless for having the *chutzpah* they lacked. Time and again he was reformed at the end by the strictures of the Hays office and the censoring code. Time and again there was the subliminal wink implying he didn't really mean it.

It was a reckless style of acting, but it suited him perfectly. Gable belonged to a time when there was still a taint of effeminacy to the acting profession. In real life, his father was a laborer who pleaded with him to come back to the oil fields where real men should be, instead of making faces on stage and screen. Even after he became a wealthy star and moved Gable Sr. down to Hollywood, the old man was never reconciled with what had become of his son. After one beer too many, his father would again goad him to give it all up and go back to a manly way of life. Gable never forgot this and became the epitome of the star who is slightly ashamed of his trade and lets everyone notice it: the type is still with us in such actors as Lee Marvin, Clint Eastwood, and Robert Mitchum.

Gable was good-looking but not obviously so. In a movie world where sound had turned sheiks into eunuchs, he was a man's man. He never preened and every time he was conscious of his own attraction he was crudely brought down by the mechanics of the film, as in *Susan Lenox,* when his seductive look at Greta Garbo is instantly mocked by the shot of a dog cocking its head at exactly the same angle.

With women, this aloofness was devastating. Gable was a master at expressing his feelings indirectly, at declaring his love a little acidly, a little ruefully. In *Wife vs. Secretary* he pretended to have forgotten his wedding anniversary and sat down to a matter-of-fact lunch with a disappointed Myrna Loy. Two or three hints about what day it was failed to pry him away from the morning paper. Then, when Loy cut the fish on her plate, there was a diamond necklace inside it. Gable loved her, but he had to hide it, to mock it, in a perennial battle to cut the sticky sentiment.

When he asked a tipsy Vivien Leigh to marry him in *Gone with the Wind,* it was almost like a business proposition and he underscored his masculine distrust of romanticism by bending his knee and performing a parody of the traditional proposal. Yet there was a constant aura of sex about him and the plots of his movies often suggested that a night with Gable was a very special experience for the girl involved.

In *Gone with the Wind* he nearly raped Vivien Leigh, who woke up next morning in singsong ecstasy. In *Lone Star,* Ava Gardner rejected him until a crucial kiss and an equally crucial fade-out: next morning she was chirping away like a liberated lark. In *Hold Your Man,* after the symbolic kiss and fade-

13

out with Gable, the camera finds a supine, morning-after Harlow, relaxed and almost totally devoid of her raucous manner. In *The Misfits,* several layers of neurosis are peeled off Marilyn Monroe as she emerges from Gable's bed in a blissful cocoon of still warm sheets. In his arms, Mary Astor lost her twitches and Grace Kelly forgot her stiff upbringing. The screen Gable insinuated he had a power to give orgasms, even to an early generation of women who still were not too sure whether they were supposed to have them.

By current standards, he could mistakenly be called the movies' first male chauvinist pig, the firm believer in the narrow ethics of *machismo.* It is a very myopic interpretation, because the Gable man despised the prim and proper concept of delicate, helpless, virginal womanhood, and gravitated towards the tough, no-nonsense, wisecracking type of female that Jean Harlow and Carole Lombard embodied.

Like Henry Higgins in *My Fair Lady,* he always seemed to be asking, "Why can't a woman be more like a man?" He was always more at ease with female co-stars he could treat like pals, in a relaxed form of sexual camaraderie. Often the women he mistreated were the ones that upheld the shackling values confronted by today's rebellious feminists. In his films, Gable did not begrudge feminine freedom, as long as it left his own masculine freedom intact.

And so the men admired him and the women loved him, this fast-talking salesman of sorely needed fantasies. He was a panacea for bruised egos. There is an exhilaration in watching Gable that sometimes has nothing to do with his films. He was a very good actor, blessed and cursed with such projection of personality that he was often accused of merely playing himself. This is not true at all: in thirty years and sixty-six films, he played Gable, a finely tuned instrument of infinite variety. It belonged to him, but it was not really he. The real Gable is another matter, another man.

In the beginning, there was this big, rather awkward chunk of a man, with huge hands, clumsy feet, and protruding ears. Even at the twilight of the golden era of romantic heroes, he was such an unlikely candidate for stardom that practically every studio head rejected him and then lived to tell the story of the one that got away, as a proof of their human fallibility.

Zanuck turned him down because of his "jug" ears. Goldwyn, not to be outdone, appropriated the story and told it as his own. Jack Warner stopped projection of a Gable screen test and gave hell to his then son-in-law Mervyn LeRoy for wasting five hundred well-earned family dollars on this "big ape." Thalberg moaned "Oh, no!" when he saw Gable as a Polynesian, complete with brown make-up, frizzy hair, and a hibiscus behind one of the prominent ears: it was in a test for *The Twain Shall Meet,* a misbegotten film Lionel Barrymore never got to direct.

According to another version, young Gable's infatuation with the theatre had come from watching a South Seas saga, *Bird of Paradise,* back in Akron, Ohio. Lionel Barrymore knew this and engineered the Polynesian test as a joke. After they all

## WHO IS GABLE, WHAT IS HE?

stopped laughing, Gable went on to the real test, a scene from his stage success *The Last Mile.* It mellowed Thalberg into giving him his first job at MGM.

There is still another version: Gable played a minor role in the Barrymore touring show, *Copperhead.* Once, on stage, his hat fell into a cardboard well and he panicked, picked it up from the fake depths, and broke up the audience, thus infuriating the crusty Barrymore. The Polynesian test was prepared by the old man in revenge against the raw amateur who had once wrecked his big scene. Years later Barrymore repented, became one of Gable's best friends and, before dying, confessed that he had wronged him cruelly and that of all the actors he knew at the time, the younger man was the only one who could play his fabled role in *Copperhead.*

The *Bird of Paradise* test is only one of the many thrice-told incidents in a life that, like *Rashomon,* takes on successive layers of fantasy. The true Gable story is buried under tons of conflicting press releases ground out

15

*THE LAST MILE. Gable in his stage role of "Killer" Mears*

over the MGM years. It is now almost impossible to sift through the myth and get to the man. Gable himself often said that the man who invented him was Howard Strickling, super-press agent and casting director of the Metro Olympus. At a glance, Strickling could tell who would be presented to the public as Venus, Jupiter, Vulcan, or Apollo.

These are, perhaps, the facts about William Clark Gable. He was born on February 1, 1901, in Cadiz, Ohio, to parents of Dutch-Irish ancestry. His frail, epileptic mother briefly survived the birth of the baby. Left with his maternal grandparents by a somewhat remorseful father, young Billy was reclaimed when Gable Sr. married Jenny Dunlap, a woman alternately described as a wicked stepmother and as a compassionate lady who channeled the boy into artistic pursuits while his father wanted him to play baseball.

All of this has to be taken with a grain of salt after the revelation that Gable's mother and father were both of pure German immigrant stock. Fearing some anti-German backlash, the Strickling office created the Dutch background for the new star, "with a dash of the Irish thrown in for good luck." When

Gable filmed *Betrayed* in Holland, he was received officially as the errant Dutchman back in the homeland. Only later did he admit to his Teutonic streak.

The standard biography goes on to tell how Jenny encouraged young Billy to leave the farm near Hopedale, Ohio, and venture into Akron. Depending on the version, he arrived there as a high school dropout of sixteen or as a high school graduate of seventeen, bent on taking premedical courses. He saw *Bird of Paradise* and was immediately bitten by the acting bug. Fatherly advice failed to cure him, for there was always Jenny helping him from afar—and now giving every Freudian apprentice a very obvious clue as to why young Gable always seemed to prefer women ten to twenty years his senior. When Jenny died, he was shaken. He joined his persistent father in Oklahoma, abandoning a stage life that had only gotten him as far as unpaid walk-ons in Akron-based touring shows.

The rigors of oil drilling turned the boy against his father's plans of making a man out of him the hard way. He fled from the wells to join a woebegone stock company called, with pathetic aspirations, the Jewell Players. He started billing himself as Clarke Gabel and often played bewigged old men, as if hiding from the scorn his father displayed against those "painted pretty boys."

In Oklahoma City he met an acting teacher, Josephine Dillon, whose main claim to fame was having once shared a Broadway stage with Edward Everett Horton. Miss Dillon was seventeen years older than Gable. She was neither rich nor influential, but she could make him an actor. He shared her poverty while she lowered his whining voice into a pleasing growl. She also recommended much-needed dental work and the gaps between his teeth began to disappear. It was still a long way off, but Billy began to look like Gable.

When Miss Dillon moved to Hollywood, he followed her to the promised land and married her in 1924. All she could do for him was to get him some jobs as an extra in such films as Lubitsch's *Forbidden Paradise* and Stroheim's *The Merry Widow*. He dropped the "e" from Clarke and rearranged Gabel into Gable, but it didn't help. He soon realized that he lacked the worldly, elegant charm of the current movie favorites and went back to the stage, where at least he could talk.

He toured with companies run by Lionel Barrymore and Jane Cowl, learned by watching them eagerly, and even got to understudy some Shakespearean parts. When he got to Broadway in Sophie Treadwell's *Machinal,* his manly presence won him good reviews and favorable audience reaction. After a middling success with Alice Brady in *Love, Honor and Betray,* his path crossed that of his future MGM alterego, Spencer Tracy. Gable watched him play in *The Last Mile,* was convinced he could never do the part in the Los Angeles production, but took it anyway. It attracted attention in Hollywood. Finally he was ready for films.

In 1930 Gable divorced Josephine Dillon and in 1931, just as he began to emerge as a star, he married Rhea Langham, a wealthy Texan. She was at least fifteen years older than he was. Rhea taught him the social graces and raised him to some low echelon in the social register. He developed a taste for expensive clothes and became something of a fashion plate. To this day, women who were enchanted by the Gable mystique in the thirties describe him by saying: "He could be a man among men, even a beast with women, but he could also act like a gentleman." Rhea Langham can be credited for the latter.

18

Life and art continued imitating each other. In early accounts of the Gable career it is difficult to separate him from the screen image of the man who pushed women around. Yet he regarded his first two wives with the awe of a pupil for a teacher and he was ultimately quite generous to them. Though Josephine Dillon neither asked for nor received a divorce settlement, Gable quietly subsidized her acting school after he became a star. From him, Rhea Langham received a then record settlement of $260,000. But he was always sensitive in this area and when he rebelled against MGM in 1933, it was because he would not accept another of "those gigolo roles."

From these two women he acquired the first elements of the Gable he was destined to become. The women he later married also contributed to the final image: Carole Lombard gave him a sense of fun and a lack of guilt in being himself, Lady Sylvia Ashley an edge of bitterness, and Kay Spreckels a middle aged contentment.

Lombard is surely the most important woman in his life. In her he found the female companion who always seemed his goal, on screen and off. They went hunting together and she camped on the ground with the men. She drank and swore with the best of them, but never lost her femininity. When she died in 1942 in a plane crash during a War Bond tour, Gable was despondent and joined the Air Force, where he displayed what has often been called suicidal courage.

After eight years of boozy loneliness, he married Lady Sylvia Ashley, Douglas Fairbanks Sr.'s ex-wife, mainly because she looked like Lombard. The resemblance was merely physical. Lady Sylvia hung chintzy curtains in Gable's ranch house and followed him on location with *Across the Wide Missouri,* only to embarrass him with clumsy ladylike efforts at rusticating, which included an unforgivably fake photograph of her dutifully cooking, with dainty, diamond-encrusted fingers.

The marriage lasted only a few months and Gable was alone again, until the last few years of his life, when he married Kay Williams Spreckels, another Lombard look alike. She mellowed him into the quiet tenderness that comes across so touchingly in his last film, *The Misfits.* Her two children called Gable "Pappy" and when he died she was pregnant. He never lived to see his only son, John

Clark Gable.

Allowing for all possible distortions, this is still a paradoxical life. A man who professed not to be an actor, just a lucky guy, nonetheless spent years of hard work learning a trade he was diffident about. On screen, he was supremely confident, but underneath he was frightened. Never forgetting his initial poverty, he feared his past and had a tendency to hide it like a half-gnawed bone.

His stinginess was legendary. He lived in mortal dread of losing his financial status. The brash adventurer of the movies was really a man who would risk nothing. Grudgingly he accepted almost every role they threw his way, never wanting to antagonize the studio powers. He married MGM and was a true organization man. When he left the studio in which he had reigned as king, it was a shattering blow on a par with an abdication.

Much as he professed to dislike his prominence, Gable truly revelled in it. Sometimes he would kid himself mercilessly.

For example, when MGM insisted that he replace his hopeless teeth with double plates, Douglas Fairbanks Sr. heard of this savory piece of news. Then jealous of the rising Gable, Fairbanks asked women how they could love the man he called "the toothless wonder." Gable knew this and once startled Mrs. Cole Porter by removing his dentures in front of her, after she had praised his gleaming smile.

He stopped joking, though, every time there was a threat to his kingly throne. It had taken him a long time to get up there and he was not going to let it go just like that. His superb timing, his off-the-cuff delivery, his infinite physical grace look so spontaneous that many forget they were painstakingly perfected through theatrical training and personal sacrifice.

It was all there, ready to rush out like the genie in the bottle, one day in late 1930 when he was asked: "Can you ride a horse?" He couldn't but he said "Sure." It was the first effective lie in Clark Gable's career.

Minna Wallis, the agent sister of producer Hal B. Wallis, had faith in Gable. Nobody else did. After unsuccessfully making the rounds all over Hollywood with her unpromising client, she took him to Pathé, where they were casting a Western, *The Painted Desert*. Riding a horse was a requisite and Gable lied without hesitation. It was his first sizable part in a film and he was paid $650 a week, more than he'd ever made before.

He took riding lessons for six weeks before the shooting started and finally learned to ride. Not that it mattered much, since the picture was short on action, long on talk. The Gable face turned out to be the only unusual feature in the picture. It was a face that rippled and rumpled, with a smile that rose diagonally, at odd angles with the mobile eyebrows. There was something feline about it and while Gable's contemporaries described him as "a handsome Jack Dempsey," he now seems more like the mischievous cat in the Hanna-Barbera "Tom and Jerry" cartoons. In his first films, he lacked the mustache that was to give a bristling edge to his Cheshire grin, but the magnetism was there.

So was the gift of distancing himself from all the absurdities

# GABLE'S FRANTIC DOZEN

of the plot, spitting inane lines out of the corner of his mouth like cherry pits after he had devoured all the pulp. In *The Painted Desert* he played a bad man with such devil-may-care truculence that he made William Boyd's hero seem doubly obtuse for not noticing that this, after all, was only a game. It was not a performance, but more a crude, unsubtle, electric defiance of the conventions. He was a villain who managed to hiss at himself.

The voice helped him immensely: a staccato delivery so inimitable that later on foreign actors engaged to dub his films were given a bonus, just for attempting the impossible. Gable machine-gunned his way into the screen with a volley of words, words, words. It was a rather small and thankless part in a bad movie, but he was launched.

*The Painted Desert* was released at the beginning of 1931, Gable's year of decision. Before it was over, twelve Gable films reached the screen and in them his image was not so much shaped as whacked into form by

21

THE PAINTED DESERT (1931). With Helen Twelvetrees and
J. Farrell MacDonald

rushing from one picture to the next. It was like speeding down the rapids in small craft, nearly overturned at every bend, keeping a miraculous balance between triumph and disaster.

He went to First National for his second film, *Night Nurse,* as a villainous chauffeur who plots to do away with two angelic and wealthy little girls. He was foiled by Barbara Stanwyck who, like Gable, was born tough. He was more earnest and less effective in this film, because William A. Wellman, the irrepressible "Wild Bill," was a firm director who would not allow any sly touches to leaven the cement-thick heavy Gable played.

In one scene he strikes Stanwyck, one of the few instances of pure cruelty towards women in his whole career. The gesture makes the otherwise foolish *Night Nurse* into a fascinating crossroads, ideal for analysis by hindsight. What would have happened to Gable if he had stayed at First National and eventually Warners? Would he have become another routine bad guy or could he have measured up to the frenzy of a Cagney or the oily brutality of a Robinson?

Equally puzzling is the way he wore a chauffeur's uniform of

22

sinister black. Seen today, Gable in *Night Nurse* is disturbingly like the young Nazis in later MGM films such as *The Mortal Storm*. Gable's family name had been anglicized from Goebel and in *Night Nurse* there is a Germanic steeliness in the eyes, an iron line to the determined jaw. His performance can only be described in metallic metaphors, and perhaps only a change in releasing schedules saved him from this bad-guy, proto-Nazi pitfall.

*Night Nurse* was held back several months and opened late in 1931, when it could no longer harm him, for he had gone the MGM way. Persistent Minna Wallis tricked Irving Thalberg into watching the Gable test with the scene from *The Last Mile*. Thalberg was still unimpressed but gave Gable a tiny part in *The Easiest Way*.

In this soap opera, the second film version of a popular play by Eugene Walter, Constance Bennett ruins her chances of marrying Robert Montgomery when she turns away from her mediocre life and is lured into becoming Adolphe Menjou's mistress. She ends up walking the streets, but in the puritanical universe of MGM thirties films it was not enough to show the

NIGHT NURSE (1931). With Ben Lyon

23

*THE EASIEST WAY (1931). With (left to right) Clara Blandick, Anita Page, Constance Bennett, J. Farrell MacDonald*

wages of sin; the rewards of virtue demanded equal time.

A new character was added in the Edith Ellis screenplay and Gable was introduced as the laundry man who married Bennett's sister, played by Anita Page. Gable was there to show the advantages of decent marriage to a working class hero, against the dangers of flirtations with rakish tycoons. Strict morality was never Gable's strong suit, but *The Easiest Way* temporarily rescued him from a lifetime of movie evil. He had little to do, but did it well in the hands of Jack Conway, a director of solid values Gable would go on to trust in the future. The performance mattered little; it was the presence that counted.

In *The Easiest Way*, Gable was the proletarian lover Depression America must have unconsciously longed for. Prosperity may not have been just around the corner, but the laundry man certainly was. If he turned out to be as handsome as Gable, who could ask for anything more? Women gobbled at the bait and MGM was deluged with letters asking who that good-looking laundry man was. Louis B. Mayer carefully withheld the reaction from Gable and signed him to a very tentative contract at $350 a week. Thalberg was still unconvinced, but Mayer was impressed by those letters and by the fact that his secretary, Ida Koverman, a sensible, middle-aged lady who was not easily shaken, had gone atwitter watching Gable's big hands in the rushes.

Despite all the omens pointing to a future leading man, the stigma of villainy was difficult to shake in Hollywood. In *Dance, Fools, Dance* he was then cast as a gangster. Joan Crawford, starting her long career as Gable's co-star, is the girl who vamps her way into his mob and becomes his favorite, but only to save her brother from the crooked path.

Gable was so memorably nasty that even in 1934, when he was already established as a romantic star, Frank Capra was dubious about casting him in *It Happened One Night,* because he still thought of him as "a gangster type." The image persisted. Right after *Dance, Fools, Dance* he was loaned to First National for another mobster role in *The Finger Points.*

In this film, directed by John Francis Dillon, Gable plays Louis Blanco, a Capone-like figure. The hero was Richard Barthelmess, clearly on the way down from Hollywood's Valhalla. Despite good photography by

Ernest Haller and some crackling lines in the John Monk Saunders screenplay, the film was routine, with none of the force of *Little Caesar* or *Public Enemy.* But Gable received good personal notices.

In this genre, the closest thing to a gangster was a reporter, for even as crusaders they had to wade into the muck they were hoping to rake. In *The Secret Six,* MGM promoted gangster Gable to the first of the many reporter parts he was to play, but the line separating both types is so tenuous that, at the time, *Film Weekly* magazine, writing

*THE EASIEST WAY (1931).* With Anita Page

*THE FINGER POINTS (1931). With Richard Barthelmess (at right)*

about *The Secret Six,* warned its readers that gangsters did not look like Clark Gable, and then went on to catalogue the traits and vices by which to recognize those evil men.

Even when Gable was fighting the mob, he was identified with them. It is an easy mistake, for in this film Gable's relationship with crime czar Wallace Beery is ambiguous indeed. Beery is Scorpio, alias "Slaughterhouse," a petty hoodlum who rises to political eminence as the power behind a venal mayor. Gable openly consorts with Scorpio, seems to accept his bribes, but is really an undercover agent for "The Secret Six," a group of influential citizens who remain anonymous behind mysterious black masks, the better to organize the war against mob rule.

It is really Wallace Beery's movie, but it is easy to see why Gable's performance caught everybody's eye. Like a frenzied chameleon, he changes colors from one scene to the next, as he steps in and out of character from brash ally of the hoodlums to staunch gang busters' apprentice. With all this activity, he finds no time to tussle with Jean Harlow, then blossoming in the sidewings as a platinum blonde, but at least they exchange a couple of sexy leers before the plot sends them both on their virtuous mission of cracking the ring.

The Gable character carries the message of the film. After one of Beery's Mafia-climbing murders, Gable beams cynically as he says, "I'm gonna make a big story out of this"; but he repents when a tearful policeman, whose son has just been "bumped off," cries: "Newspapermen keep making heroes out of hoodlums." From that point his course is clear, and his confrontation with the masked "Secret Six" has a ritualistic solemnity out of the "Dick Tracy" serials. Through all this, there is the endless wonder of hearing the multiple inflections Gable could get out of a then current idiom like "Oh, yeah?" He makes it range from sexy to menacing to complaisant, with countless shadings in between.

*The Secret Six* is an odd film. Director George Hill was evidently impressed by the German cinema and he diluted some of the heavier tricks to make them palatable for mass audiences. It is a tortuous, sometimes brilliant picture, filled with strong echoes of Fritz Lang and equipped with a sinister deaf-mute who even resembles Peter Lorre.

Though its intentions were aggressively moralistic and its vio-

THE SECRET SIX (1931). On the set with (left to right) Jean Harlow, Wallace Beery, and unidentified actress

*LAUGHING SINNERS (1931). With Joan Crawford*

lence tame by today's standards, *The Secret Six* was considered a bloody film, and was bitterly accused of glamorizing the underworld. It was censored and cut to shreds, as well as banned outright in New Jersey, where it supposedly inspired a child to shoot a playmate while playing "Secret Six" with loaded guns. It created a furor and its rather notorious success persuaded Gable to stay in films, instead of returning to the more refined stage work preferred by Rhea Langham, whom he had just married.

His star was moving fast, though it was difficult to chart its rise in the crowded MGM heavens. But when a star fell, it happened so quickly that no one had time to even make a wish on it. John Mack Brown, who had played Gable's sidekick in *The Secret Six,* had just finished *Laughing Sinners* with Joan Crawford. The audience had liked the Gable-Crawford combination in *Dance, Fools, Dance* and the studio thought nothing of discarding all the Mack Brown footage and replacing him with Gable.

It must have given Gable a clue that his fortunes were rising, but it was a hollow victory. He was cast as a Salvation Army worker who redeemed Crawford from becoming the mistress of a roué, played by Neil Hamilton. The two men could have exchanged roles to each other's advantage.

In today's hit-or-miss star market, *Laughing Sinners* could have scuttled Gable, but in his year of the decisive dozen, the tempo was hit and run. His big break came directly afterwards, when Norma Shearer, Thalberg's wife, requested Gable for *A Free Soul.* Acting with the boss's wife was the equivalent of marrying the boss's daughter and *A Free Soul* was a landmark in Gable's progress.

Shearer was always mindful of her demure image, to the point of even rationalizing the impossibility of her playing Scarlett O'Hara by claiming that her fan mail advised her against accepting such a bitchy role. In *A Free Soul* she plays Lionel Barrymore's spoiled rich daughter, who spurns the gentle and pallid Leslie Howard to have an affair with hoodlum Gable. She hates herself for stooping so low, but she loves it too, as the first of the screen women who were liberated by orgasm in Gable's career as Metro's prize stud.

When Shearer lies back languorously on a couch, encircles Gable in her arms, and brazenly purrs "Come on, put them

29

*A FREE SOUL (1931). With Norma Shearer*

around me," there was little doubt what was going on. She subsequently utters a line that was prophetic for the Gable myth: "A new man, a new world." It was the first of Gable's many films with Clarence Brown, a director who understood the star's attraction and let him suggest it tactfully, never grossly. *A Free Soul* was really about erotic awakening, but of course everyone paid dearly for all the fun.

Gable's high spot in the film came by accident. Thalberg saw the rushes and feared this supporting player was stealing the show from the stars, so he inserted a scene in which Gable slaps Shearer, to divert audience sympathy from him. The audience loved it. Lionel Barrymore won the Academy Award as Norma's outraged father who shoots Gable, but it was Gable who stayed in people's minds.

His next film, *Sporting Blood*, did not further his career. It was a minor opus in which he played a smiling but crooked racetrack character and it was released in August, 1931, on the same day as the delayed *Night Nurse*. They were both mercifully swept under the carpet by his steam-

30

roller wave of popularity after *A Free Soul.* With this film, Gable's fate was sealed. MGM was a matriarchy and suddenly every woman on the lot wanted the Gable treatment, as an acid test of the Ying and Yang celluloid folly.

Garbo failed the test. She asked for Gable in *Susan Lenox: Her Fall and Rise,* and he was given a John Gilbert part as a suave engineer. The chemistry was all wrong between them. Garbo never really said "I want to be alone," but she seems to be thinking along these lines when ever one of her co-stars becomes an unwelcome intruder in her own private world. In *Susan Lenox,* Gable has to parry with

Garbo as a fallen virgin who joins the circus, becomes a kept woman, and hits rock-bottom in a Panamanian brothel. Even there she still has the audacity to imply she is some kind of innocent bystander who never joins the festivities.

It is difficult to take all this with a straight face and the film offers fascinating glimpses of Gable's reactions. Garbo's upstaging antics drive him from exasperation to unbridled fury. In scene after scene, she has the kind of dead-end lines that can only be answered with an obscenity. After Garbo sneakily dampens the effect of his drinking bout tirade with a marvelously dolorous gesture of cover-

*SPORTING BLOOD (1931). With Madge Evans*

*SUSAN LENOX, HER FALL AND RISE (1931). With Greta Garbo*

ing his glass with her trembling hand, Gable goes into a tantrum that now seems not entirely the character's. He stomps out, grabs a persistent prostitute who has been propositioning him and flings her down a flight of stairs into the bar. It is very possible that he had Garbo-Lenox in mind. He had his vengeance, though. In the last scene, when Garbo declaims "We are two cripples clinging to each other for salvation," he looks her straight in the eye and sneers: "You have a very queer view of things."

It was their one and only film together. Garbo was an emanation from a gauzy era. She still ambled about, deliciously ghost-like, vainly searching around a movie crypt for the shades of Antonio Moreno, Ramon Novarro, and all her dear departed lovers. Gable represented the upsurging realism that put her out of her misery and into an inaccessible pantheon.

Actually, Crawford was a greater danger for Gable. In *Possessed,* it took all of Clarence Brown's sense of pacing to crowd the story into seventy-three minutes. Gable was a lawyer with political aspirations, harmed by the woman he loved: Crawford, an ex-laborer in a box factory. She has to be kept out of the public eye until she acquires polish, but both the liaison and her past are brought up by hecklers at a political rally. To save Gable's future, Crawford stands up and reveals that she has already left him. The crowd relents and cheers them, and they are presumably on their way to the gubernatorial mansion.

Crawford heroines of the thirties, with their barely disguised trashiness, were a threat to the vital frankness of the Gable heroes. There is an inherent hypocrisy that infects the women she played, and it works against the sincerity he was so good at. In *Possessed*, the Crawford character could only be believable if a very shady past were provided by the screenplay. By laundering it, the film implied, in a quaint aristocratic twist, that a working class girl was ineligible as the wife of a man seeking office.

The audience did not realize it was being insulted indirectly and joined in applauding Craw-

*POSSESSED (1931). With Joan Crawford*

*HELL DIVERS (1931). With Wallace Beery*

ford for bettering herself and Gable for not holding that box factory against her. *Possessed* did well and spawned further pictures in which Crawford forced Gable into feats of bogus nobility for her sake.

*Hell Divers,* Gable's last release in that hectic 1931, was directed by George Hill of *The Secret Six* and was based, like *Test Pilot* in 1938, on an original story by Lt. Commander Frank Wead. *Hell Divers* did not amount to much. The effort to develop a Quirt-Flagg relationship in the style of *What Price Glory* failed in the Gable-

Wallace Beery team. They had worked successfully as antagonists in *The Secret Six,* but Gable was too competitive a screen figure, and he involuntarily exuded a sex appeal that made his sidekicks look older, uglier, and duller. The jovial palship these films needed was only achieved—up to a point— with the Tracy-Gable films.

By the end of 1931, after a dozen movies in a year, the results on the Gable election must have been coming in: he was enormously popular with both men and women, and he possessed a devilish sense of humor to temper his undoubted mean streak. It all seems clear now, yet MGM, the legendary studio that hatched and nurtured stars, still had no idea of what they had stumbled into. Despite the evidence of a dozen films, they put him in *Polly of the Circus*.

It was shot late in 1931 and released early in 1932, to make up a Gable baker's dozen. Marion Davies wanted Gable and William Randolph Hearst made sure to get him for her. Hearst's Cosmopolitan Pictures were released through MGM and Gable was offered to Davies' sacrificial altar. No one could shake Hearst's concept of his star protégée as a vestal virgin. Gable, with his reputation as a sizzling and arousing cinema lover, had to be spayed before he even got near her. They had him play a pious rector who loses his church and congregation when he marries a trapeze artist, played by Davies. She was, of course, the purest thing under the big top and Bishop C. Aubrey Smith finally gives them his blessing.

Even patient, dutiful Gable, still awed by his newborn stardom, felt that *Polly of the Circus* was a giant step in the wrong direction. He stayed away from the set for a few days, but

*POLLY OF THE CIRCUS (1932). With Marion Davies*

*POLLY OF THE CIRCUS (1932). On the set with director Alfred Santell and Marion Davies*

he was finally brought back by a raise of several hundred dollars more a week. That his career survived *Polly of the Circus* is again proof of his indestructible power. No one could wipe him out. Not even the combined forces of Hearst, Mayer, and Davies. Not even Clark Gable.

Gable initially refused to star in nearly all of his memorable films. *Red Dust* (1932) was no exception. He felt the studio was punishing him for staging a small rebellion against *Polly of the Circus* by pairing him with Jean Harlow, whom the critics had thus far singled out as a no-talent blonde. He found *Red Dust* vulgar and thought Harlow's reputation as a screen gun moll would remind audiences of the gangster films he had left behind.

He accepted the film reluctantly, persuaded by Victor Fleming—a director he trusted—and also by fear of suspension of his contract at MGM. The screenplay by John Lee Mahin, based on a play by Wilson Collison, has Harlow as a prostitute escaping the police and seeking refuge in a rubber plantation run by Gable in Indochina. Afraid she may cause dissension among the men who covet her, he agrees to let her stay only until the next boat arrives to take her away. Despite his rough dismissal of the girl, he begins to find her charming and resourceful, even when she uses the drinking water to take a sexy bath in a barrel.

When Gene Raymond, an engineer, arrives with his wife, Mary Astor, she and Gable are

# THE WINDING WAY TO OSCAR

immediately attracted to each other. Gable sends Raymond to build a bridge in the jungle and starts having an affair with Astor, though he is repelled by her capacity for deceit. When the husband comes back, Gable decides to get away from her by pretending to favor Harlow. With all the fury of a woman scorned, Astor shoots him, though not fatally. Quick-witted Harlow convinces the baffled husband that she had seen Astor defending her honor against caddish Gable. Raymond and Astor leave; Gable and Harlow stay together.

A brief synopsis conveys little of what the stars brought to *Red Dust*. Here, Gable and Harlow met at last in the right ring for the perfect match. The Hays office refereed the bout with one eye closed, and the braless goddess more than measured up to the man who was to change American fashion in men's wear by discarding undershirts. The two sex symbols clashed and clanged, making beautiful music together.

Their screen personalities

*RED DUST (1932). Gable rehearsing lines*

*RED DUST (1932). With (left to right) Donald Crisp, Gene Raymond, Mary Astor, Jean Harlow*

dovetailed so precisely that *Red Dust* became a high point in the history of movie erotica, thirties style. Not that it was easy for the Gable character to instantly recognize his symbiotic relationship with Harlow's. He was playing the archetypical man of his times, still steeped in waning Victorian ideals about enjoying the company of loose women like Harlow, but hankering after the mentally corseted charms of well-bred Astor.

*Red Dust* was a sexual Horatio Alger story with a two-way ticket for the hero. He temporar-ily followed the road up to Astor, but deep down he knew there was no place like Harlow's, even though her house was not exactly a home. Very early in the game, Harlow's intuition told her she held the winning cards, and she played them with hilariously raffish bravado. She streetwalked through the picture with confidence that no one could take a man like Gable away from her.

The Gable-Astor-Harlow triangle certified Gable as the would-be gentleman who is briefly impressed by ladies but

RED DUST (1932). On the set with (left to right) Mary Astor, Gene
Raymond, director Victor Fleming, Donald Crisp

enduringly amused by golden-hearted tarts. In Harlow's tarnished heroine, Gable's raunchy hero found the ideal female pal he could enjoy sex with as an added bonus. It is a fantasy of male eternal and *Red Dust* inevitably broke box-office records. Also inevitably, after several runs in regular theatres, it played in burlesque houses.

None of this pleased Clark Gable. In real life, he was more difficult to win over than the man he portrayed. Recurrently, in an often repeated chord in his life and career, he was both pleased and ashamed by the success of *Red Dust*. He much preferred a contemporary film that gave him a taste of the prestige he desired so vehemently.

Norma Shearer, whom he had slapped in *A Free Soul,* got back at him with Eugene O'Neill's *Strange Interlude* (1932). The

*STRANGE INTERLUDE (1932). As aging Ned Darrell*

part of Nina gave her the perfect emasculating weapon. Nina is unquestionably the most efficient castrator the American theatre ever produced, and no mean contender for international honors against Hedda Gabler and the Strindberg women. As Ned Darrell, her constant lover, Gable played one of the prize fools in stage history with a sorrowful restraint that proved how good he could be in a part he deeply respected, however miscast he might have been in it.

In *Strange Interlude* he is literally put to stud by Nina-Shearer, who marries a wealthy man with a family streak of insanity and then decides to have a healthy child by Darrell-Gable. The son is passed off as her husband's and grows up to hate his real father. Gable aged convincingly through all this, suffering silently as Shearer's household pet, discreetly altered as soon as he had produced the desired offspring.

The screenplay preserved the O'Neill theatrical ploy of having the characters voice their inner thoughts as asides, and director Robert Z. Leonard availed himself of the chance to prove how effective films can be for soliloquy. Leonard was not a rigorous director and the players seem left on their own during these tricky scenes. Shearer and especially Ralph Morgan make faces, as if they were attempting to suit the gesture to the prerecorded lines they were hearing on the set. It is a technique that gives *Strange Interlude* the odd air of a silent film with added and extraneous comments. Soon the mouth-twitching and eye-rolling become laughable.

Gable alone had the restraint to listen to his own words and regard them not as cues for grimaces but as thoughts to be hidden with an impassive countenance. His performance is light-years ahead of the others in technique, and can be credited to his own intuition since Leonard was letting everyone else emote into a paroxysm.

Shallow though it ultimately is, the film at least accomplished the job of compressing a five-hour play into 110 minutes of straight narrative. Robert Z. Leonard was hardly an imaginative director but his work in *Strange Interlude* was merely carpentry; he judiciously hacked away to reduce O'Neill's baroque credenza of a play into a convenient lowboy of a movie.

Gable's solid, painfully passive performance must have gratified his ego as an actor. It added an illusion of artistic stature to his career and it also

42

*STRANGE INTERLUDE* (1932). With Norma Shearer

*STRANGE INTERLUDE* (1932). With Ralph Morgan and Alexander Kirkland

STRANGE INTERLUDE (1932). On the set with Norma Shearer, with
Robert Z. Leonard directing

added the mustache that was to
be his trademark. The mustache
did not yet quiver with anger or
disdain, but it was there for the
first time, bringing together the
asymmetrical face.

Like a king in exile, Gable
found his brightest moments
when he could get away from the
pomp and circumstance of the
MGM court. He was loaned to
Paramount for *No Man of Her
Own* (1932) with Carole Lombard, and he swam with ease in

the goldfish bowl of the studio
renowned for sophisticated and
screwball comedies. Sensible
Lombard was infinitely better
at taming Gable than those
highstrung Metro girls.

In *No Man of Her Own*, Gable
plays a runaway gambler and
Lombard a small-town librarian.
He marries her on the flip of a
coin but soon she applies the
light touch and slowly puts him
through the wringer of a nine-to-
five routine, in the kind of

snappy sequence director Wesley Ruggles was particularly good at handling.

Even at Paramount's carefree empire, Gable had to be made an honest man by the time the folks were sent home from the theatre. He renounces his crooked ways, serves a ninety-day sentence, and comes back to Lombard, not wholly reconstructed but at least pleasantly renovated. Even so, the film managed to avoid the heavy-handed repentance that clogged those MGM last reels, with their instant conversions of scamps and vamps.

For Gable, after his Paramount fling, it was back to the drawing board at MGM. He was costarred with Helen Hayes, one of the few actresses who can claim to have been born a little

*NO MAN OF HER OWN (1932). With Carole Lombard*

THE WHITE SISTER (1933). With Helen Hayes

old lady. In *The White Sister* (1933), she was the ethereal nun Gable tries to seduce away from the convent. The Gable blowtorch style could by then melt an iceberg, but not Helen Hayes in a nun's habit. On a television talk show in 1971, the actress reminisced about Gable and how ashamed the poor man was of his big, scarred hands. Perennially in awe of *grandes dames,* he must have felt he was not good enough to touch her. All through the film, an invisible ten-foot pole seems to be keeping them apart, even when they embrace.

*Night Flight* (1933), his other film with Hayes, is inconsequential to Gable's career. Here, he was a pilot trying to get air mail into Paris, while his wife (Hayes) fretted at home and tangled with the Barrymores (John and Lionel) on the necessity of flying in treacherous darkness just to deliver a letter one day sooner. This was one of the early MGM prestige films, where an all-star cast could be arranged by asking several contract players to drop in on the set for a couple of afternoons' shooting. Myrna Loy and Robert Montgomery are also in *Night Flight*. A film like this could make strange bedfellows and after finishing his scheduled week in some picture, a player could find himself on the marquee with someone he'd never seen on the set, from Marie Dressler to Harpo Marx.

*Night Flight* was directed by Clarence Brown and received admiring reviews, because the aerial scenes were technically interesting for 1932. It was merely full of names and hot air and Gable, forced to sit throughout his performance in the cockpit of a plane, was totally wasted. The only rewarding role was John Barrymore's as the obsessed man who rigidly insists on the flights. In one of those permutations of personality that turn movie stardom into musical chairs, Gable would play a variation of this role fifteen years later, in *Command Decision*.

NIGHT FLIGHT (1933). As pilot Jules Fabian

In 1933, MGM should have tried to recreate the Gable-Harlow chemistry that had stirred all that *Red Dust*. Instead, they were cast in *Hold Your Man* (1933), a film so at odds with their potential that it now seems almost a deliberate attempt to sabotage them. But *Hold Your Man* was not made in hatred for its stars; just in fear of their implications.

Moralistic pressures were strong. America was in the depths of the Depression and austere times demand clean or at least deodorized idols. It has often been assumed that Gable and Harlow were ripe for consumption at precisely the moment their popularity as a team reached its zenith. Psychologically they may have been, but not sociologically. What audiences may have wanted to see is one thing. What they were allowed to be shown is quite another.

Paul Bern, Harlow's husband, had committed suicide in bizarre circumstances during the shooting of *Red Dust*. Several vigilante groups were up in arms to ban Harlow from the screen, so MGM had to salvage a profitable star property at all costs.

In *The Last Tycoon*, F. Scott Fitzgerald's novel about Hollywood, there is a passage in which Monroe Starr, the Thalberg prototype, demands revisions of a photoplay in production. The girl is a Harlowish temptress and Starr insists that, whatever the girl may do in the early reels, she has to be toned down later, so she can be regarded as "a future mother." Fitzgerald had worked on the Harlow screenplay for *Red Headed Woman* and was certainly aware of what went on behind the Metro palace stairs. At any rate, this attitude toward Harlow found its way into *Hold Your Man,* and the result is a curiously schizophrenic movie.

The film starts fast and furious, with Gable as a petty swindler fleeing the police and invading Harlow's apartment. She does not know him from Adam but, like Eve eternal, she helps him out with the recklessness of instant lust. Policemen knock on the door and Gable is already in the bathtub, fully soaped into an unrecognizable mask. Harlow claims the stranger is her husband and the cops leave. Gable has only taken off his shirt to step hurriedly into the tub, so his pants have to be quick-dried in the oven. He moves around the apartment in a bathrobe and the atmosphere of cheap sex is heady as he examines the tawdry trophies on

48

Harlow's wall: a veritable palimpsest of Atlantic City banners, fly-specked kewpie dolls, and other mementos of weekend paramours, including photos of sailors, marines, and firemen.

As in *Red Dust,* she becomes the aggressor, he the diffident prey. The next step is logically the bedroom, but Gable flees on hearing another knock on the door. Harlow does not give up and starts frequenting his favorite cabaret. They meet again, he calls her "sweetmeat" and lewdly presses against her in a ruttish fox trot. Their conversation becomes dizzyingly sexy. To Gable's "I'll grow on you," Harlow replies, "Yeah, like a carbuncle." About to leave his apartment, in a last-ditch attempt at pathetic defensiveness, she sneers, "I got what I came here for," and he leers, "Are you sure?"

They become lovers but when Harlow fears she can no longer hold her man, she taunts him with the imminent visit of an admirer, a respectably married man from out of town. The stage is set for the badger game but when Gable storms into the apartment, pretending to be Harlow's outraged brother, he has an inexplicable change of heart. Instead of blackmailing the fall guy, he punches him and

informs Harlow that from now on she will only kiss *him*. To insure it, they immediately run out to get a marriage license but when they come back the whole block is swarming with cops. Gable's unlucky punch has killed the man, in a death as accidental as their own sudden virtue. He runs away, Harlow takes the rap and is sent to a conventlike prison.

*Hold Your Man* must have started as a sleazy comedy-melodrama with a strong whiff of *Double Indemnity* and other forties forays into the aphrodisiac powers of partnership in crime. The times were not yet ripe for that, so the picture had to canonize Harlow and whitewash Gable. In jail she discovers she's going to have a child and as soon as Gable finds out the movie shrivels like a fetus in a formaldehyde bottle.

When Gable visits Harlow in prison, the film aims at some last-minute suspense on whether they can get married in the chapel before the police arrive to get a hold on him. "Give my kid a chance," Gable begs the preacher, lamely pleading for an ideal of legitimacy. They barely make it, but the baby is saved from the cliff-hanging danger of being born a bastard. "It must have been the Lawd who ordered

*HOLD YOUR MAN (1933). With Jean Harlow*

it," moans the Negro church man out of *The Green Pastures*: MGM was touching all the bases with this one. The last sequence has Gable, Harlow, and baby boy reunited and on their way to straight living in Cincinnati.

*Hold Your Man* is, without a doubt, the nadir of Gable's career. It is very easy to laugh at the conventions of the period, but it is more fitting to lament them. From the vantage point of today's liberal screen mores, it seems a sad waste that this virile man and this pungent woman had to enact such hypocritical charades. Even at the end of the decade, Gable had to get the equivalent of a papal dispensation from the Hays office to say "I don't give a damn" at the conclusion of *Gone with the Wind.* Harlow never reached that point. *Hold Your Man* was not a vehicle for them. It was a chastity belt.

His next assignment, *Dancing*

*Lady* (1933), was too much even for Gable. Joan Crawford played the title role and he was miscast in an exact equivalent of the Warner Baxter part in Warners' *42nd Street*. Gable's role was meager and the screenplay an incubator to warmed-over clichés such as "Hey, that kid has talent" and "Go out there and show them you're a star."

To his immense credit, *Dancing Lady* proves how awkward and ill at ease Gable was in things now called "campy." The film was a cheap dress rehearsal for what would eventually become the spectacular, vaudeville-oriented MGM musicals using the Ziegfeld name: *The Great Ziegfeld* (1936), *Ziegfeld Girl* (1941), and *Ziegfeld Follies* (1946).

When Gable was not amused, he was capable of performances close to the high W. C. Fields count of irritability, with none of the covert humor. In *Dancing*

*HOLD YOUR MAN (1933). With director Sam Wood*

*DANCING LADY (1933). With Joan Crawford*

*Lady,* with Nelson Eddy, Fred Astaire, and even the Three Stooges cavorting around him, he was furious. At one point, Crawford remarked that she had seen his angry face backstage and wondered if she was doing something wrong. She was, in fact, dancing abominably, but that was not what the Gable character was supposed to convey, so he merely muttered, "Maybe I have that kind of a face."

After finishing *Dancing Lady,* Gable went into the hospital to recover from exhaustion, to have an appendectomy, and to get rid of the last of his hopeless teeth. He stayed away long enough to be accused of malingering. A ten-week vacation was unheard of at the Metro assembly line. When he came back to assert he would never again make a picture like the last one, Louis B.

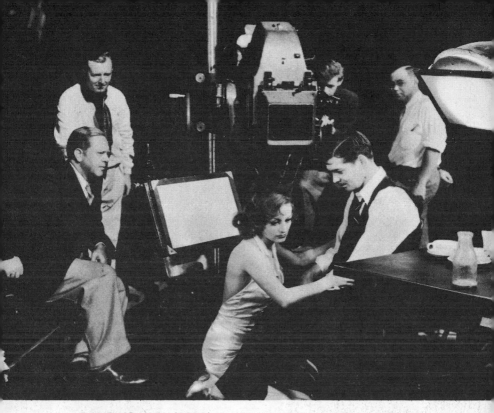

Mayer had the right punishment for this upstart. It turned out to be *It Happened One Night*.

He would never have gotten that kind of break on home ground at Culver City. The original story, "Night Bus" by Samuel Hopkins Adams, had appeared in *Cosmopolitan* magazine, a Hearst publication. Since Hearst's Cosmopolitan Pictures were released through MGM, Mayer had first refusal

rights and he turned it down. The blustering, plutocratic father figure, eventually played by Walter Connolly, was presented in too harsh a light, according to Mayer. The film, of course, would have helped Marion Davies enormously, but Hearst could not see his darling running away from middle-aged authority in a cross-country escape.

"Night Bus" was careening into oblivion when it was hi-

Gable at premiere of GRAND HOTEL with (left to right) Norma Shearer, Irving Thalberg, and Rhea Langham, his second wife

jacked by Frank Capra and Robert Riskin, who started a story treatment for Columbia. Capra had to abandon the project when Harry Cohn, the incumbent tyrant at Columbia, sent him to Metro to direct *Soviet,* an oddity that was to have Gable as an American engineer building a dam in Russia.

Mayer had found a fabulously vindictive three-way ploy. Thalberg's recurrent heart trouble had forced him to take a long vacation in Europe. Holding the studio reins firmly in his hands, Mayer cancelled *Soviet,* a Thalberg project, and sent Capra, whom he could not abide, back to Columbia. With him he sent Gable, who quickly went from *Soviet* to Siberia, as they called Harry Cohn's poverty row studio on the other side of the Hollywood tracks. Exile would teach Gable to appreciate the joys of Metro, where Father Mayer always knew best.

Crafty Louis B. Mayer knew that the only picture Capra had ready for Gable was his rejected "Night Bus." He also knew that MGM had just released *Fugitive Lovers,* a Robert Montgomery "bus" picture that had flopped, presumably draining the market for anything similar. In self defense, Capra and Riskin were backing away from the project. Gable was getting drunk in despair. The only man in Hollywood who wanted to go ahead with "Night Bus" was Harry Cohn, because he had nothing else for Gable and Capra.

Gable was not alone in shying away from "Night Bus." Miriam Hopkins, Myrna Loy, Margaret Sullavan, and Constance Bennett had all turned it down. Finally Claudette Colbert accepted, punished by Paramount according to the old version or out of greed according to the Capra version: she was promised a full salary for making a film in four weeks and not one day over.

Nothing that went on before the first shot seems to matter. Released early in 1934, *It Happened One Night* was a genuine event. It is as if the film had been waiting in limbo, to be born of a piece the very instant the cameras started rolling. The definitive Gable was also waiting there, ready to step into his own at the first crack of the sound board.

There have been many great performances in films, but few transcendental ones. Gable's in *It Happened One Night* is one of them. Just as Brando's hip-slouching, mumbling manner in *The Wild One* prefigured the Beats, Hippies, and all forthcoming rebels, Gable in *It Hap-*

55

pened *One Night* set the mold for the man of the thirties and forties.

His impact was shattering. Women all over America coined a phrase that sounded like a press agent's dream: "Who do you think you are? Clark Gable?" It meant he was the ultimate in masculinity and men got the message. They tried to imitate his brashness, his skepticism, his secretive tenderness. Gable became paragon to a whole generation and World War II sent the image parading all over the world. Even now, when a foreign film tries very hard to present a caricature of "the typical American," there are traces of Gable in the bogus portrait.

In *It Happened One Night,* Gable distilled the mannerisms of the thirties in the way he snapped down the brim of his hat or slung his jacket over his shoulder. He was a study in unconsciously artful pantomime, teaching refined Claudette Colbert to dunk a doughnut, giving her an object lesson on how a man undresses, or a classic demonstration of hitchhiking techniques.

Capra shot most of the movie on the road, with a great deal of improvisation, adapting the bright ideas in Robert Riskin's screenplay to whatever they found on the way, adding new touches inspired by the fresh locations. It was a style of moviemaking that proved ideal for Gable. Often on his own, moving in full shots and long takes as in the hitchhiking scene, he combined unwavering masculinity with almost ballet-like physical grace.

Free from the constriction of Cedric Gibbons sets, MGM soft lighting, and discreetly glossy medium shots, he moved like a dynamo from head to toe. Few other actors are capable of giving themselves to a role not only with their faces but with their whole bodies, as Gable did in *It Happened One Night.*

Gable's ideal director was Capra, a man who said, "My characters do what human beings would do if they had the courage or the opportunity." That's Gable all right. Furthermore, Capra obliterated the distinction between hero and comic. To Gable, he gave routines that only slapstick comedians had tried before. Suddenly it was a discovery to be able to laugh at the man you loved or admired. It had been done for centuries in reality, but it was a novelty with romantic screen idols.

The plot of *It Happened One Night* was tailor-made for Gable,

*IT HAPPENED ONE NIGHT (1934). With Claudette Colbert*

crystallizing all the fine chemical components in his personality. He plays a jobless reporter who tells his boss off and then luckily stumbles into a great story: a runaway heiress defying her father after he had annulled her marriage to a fortune hunter. In return for an exclusive story, Gable promises to help the girl get from Miami to New York, back to her shifty husband in name only.

In transit, Gable is forced to protect his scoop by going through a repertoire of character parts. He pretends to be a menacing, kidnapping gangster just to frighten away Roscoe Karns, who has recognized Colbert and wants to share the loot. He goes into a Jiggs and Maggie fight with Colbert to deceive snooping agents into believing they are just another average, quarreling married couple.

All the way to the end, he is spectacularly materialistic. He does not want the girl, just the story, and so they raise the unforgettable "walls of Jericho" by stringing a sheet between their two motel beds. Yet he has a deeply hidden romantic core and dreams of an island he once saw and has never been able to forget. He was all the Gables, past and future, rolled into one.

He won an Oscar for this performance. Colbert, Capra, and Riskin also received Academy Awards and *It Happened One Night* was chosen as the best film of 1934, the only one in history to have made such a clean sweep of Academy honors. It had opened early in the year, to no great critical acclaim. It was neither created nor received as a classic. It just became one. It was a natural, an original, an accident, a miracle. Like Clark Gable.

In a lecture at the National Film Theatre in London, James Stewart said that film stars often based their impact on "good moments" in a few films. Remembered over the years, these moments can add up to insure an actor's career as a star. Hepburn caressing the calla lilies in *Stage Door;* Bogart reminiscing to "As Time Goes By" in *Casablanca;* Cooper walking down an empty street in *High Noon;* Stewart himself, collapsing on the Senate floor in *Mr. Smith Goes to Washington.* Each moviegoer treasures his own favorites. They live in memory, sometimes more vividly than the quickly forgotten minutiae of everyday life.

From 1934, when he made *It Happened One Night,* to 1941, when he left Hollywood to enlist in the Air Force, Gable accumulated enough of those memorable moments to last him a lifetime. Also, among the twenty-four films he starred in during that period, several are better than the sum of their inspired Gable parts.

In 1934, Gable had not yet won the Oscar many were predicting for him in *It Happened One Night,* but his performance under Capra's direction had convinced MGM that he had talent beyond his box-office popularity.

# ALL HAIL THE KING

Local boy had made good at Columbia and when he came back to the Culver City home lot there was a plum part in a prestige movie waiting for him.

Gable was cast in *Men in White* (1934), Waldemar Young's adaptation of Sidney Kingsley's Pulitzer prize play. Under Richard Boleslawski's direction, he played a young doctor torn between the superficial lure of a brittle and wealthy fiancée (Myrna Loy) and the selfless example set by an idealistic old doctor (Jean Hersholt). Gable is required to operate on the young nurse he had seduced (Elizabeth Allan).

In close-up, the play's operating room suspense became heavily melodramatic. *Film Daily* hailed the arrival of a "new" Gable who did not battle the ladies, but audiences were indifferent to the film, and Gable's plum part turned bitter as a persimmon. His stern nobility was not successful, so the studio sent him back to where he had started: a gangster part.

This time he was a *good* gangster. In *Manhattan Melodrama*

*MEN IN WHITE (1934). With Myrna Loy*

(1934), the first of his films under W. S. Van Dyke's direction, he goes nobly to the electric chair, knowing that his death will save the marriage and career of his ex-love (Myrna Loy) and his childhood friend (William Powell), an exemplary man who has managed to conquer poverty and become district attorney. Mickey Rooney played Gable as a boy, and the picture was one of the many variations of a favorite Depression plot: two ghetto children parting at the crossroads,

one to take the high road to virtue and the other the low road to vice. To increase audience sympathy, *Manhattan Melodrama* threw in a third boy who took the shortcut to heaven by becoming a priest (Leo Carrillo).

Its sentimentality snared even professionals: *Manhattan Melodrama* was the movie Dillinger had gone to see in Chicago on the night he was shot by the FBI as he left the theatre. A publicity break like that was a press agent's dream and it was exploited by news items stating that Dillinger was such a fan of the Gable-Loy team that he could not bear missing the film, even at the risk of his life. With all this going for it, *Manhattan Melodrama* was a success, but it did not save Gable from again falling into the clutches of his next leading lady: the redoubtable Joan Crawford.

Their clashing values as a movie team were incidentally defined in *Broadway Melody of 1938*, when Judy Garland sang "You Made Me Love You" to a photograph of "Dear Mr. Gable." In a recitative between choruses, Garland gushed: "And then in that picture with Joan Crawford, I cried and cried because you loved her so much and you couldn't have her . . . not until the end of the picture, anyway." Garland was mildly caricaturing what the Gable fans seemed to want—their hero as the ever resourceful pursuer of the temporarily unavailable Crawford.

Yet starting with *Chained* (1934), the Gable characters progressively became stronger, the better to control what critic Parker Tyler astutely defined as "Joan Crawford's vocation for tragedy." In *Chained,* Gable meets Crawford during a cruise, when she is running away in despair from Otto Kruger, who

MANHATTAN MELODRAMA (1934). With Myrna Loy

*CHAINED (1934). With Stuart Erwin and Joan Crawford*

couldn't have her because he was already married. On the rebound from Kruger she falls in love with Gable, but when she comes back to reveal her change of heart, Kruger has already sacrificed his marriage and Crawford is shackled into making an honest man of him.

John Lee Mahin, who had written the screenplay for *Red Dust*, again made the Gable character more forceful in *Chained*. Gable would have none of this sacrificial Crawford non-

sense and she was his at the end, leaving Kruger in the lurch. Clarence Brown made a dream of a woman's picture, reassuring many a wife with its implications that it served Kruger right to lose Crawford, since no middle-aged gentleman should leave home and hearth to enter into fruitless competition with Gable.

It was not until their next film, *Forsaking All Others* (1934), that Gable really gained the upper hand in the confronta-

CHAINED (1934). On the set with director Clarence Brown

tion of Gable-Crawford movie styles as snickering man and weeping lady. A good Joseph L. Mankiewicz screenplay, snappily directed by W. S. Van Dyke, presents Gable as a patient beau who knew Crawford was not bad, merely capricious: she would finally see the light and favor him over Robert Montgomery.

Gable was very good in a sardonic comedy role and *Forsaking All Others* is that paradox: a memorable movie that few remember, except for the "good moment" that caps it. In the last scene he is sailing away from Crawford, finally resigned to leave her with Montgomery. He had made a point that she needed a good thrashing and as he enters his cabin on the ship he is surprised to find her with extended hand, offering him the back of the brush for the required spanking. It amounted to a T. K. O. victory of Gable over Crawford.

*After Office Hours* (1935) teamed Gable with Constance

*FORSAKING ALL OTHERS (1934)*. With Joan Crawford

Bennett in the newspaper milieu Herman J. Mankiewicz' screenplays so lovingly and knowingly caught, down to the last wisecrack and inflection. Bennett is a socialite who wants to be a reporter but is fired by editor Gable. He rehires her upon finding out she can be used to get the inside dope on a promisingly juicy divorce scandal.

Unscrupulously he manipulates the girl to get the front page story and when she gets involved in a murder plot, Gable gets an even bigger scoop. It is, at bottom, not a very sympathetic part and though reviewers accused him of burlesquing it, he was shrewdly coating the bitter pill with his sense of humor. Under Robert Z. Leonard's absent-minded direction Gable had a chance to introduce a lot of sly fun and *After Office Hours* shows Gable's cunning Brechtian trick of placing some distance between himself and his role.

He was then loaned by MGM

to Twentieth Century, later to become 20th Century-Fox. Louis B. Mayer had invested in the budding studio to help his son-in-law William B. Goetz into a better position at its helm and also to keep his fingers in as many Hollywood pies as possible. Farming out a star was considered mildly degrading, but Gable was easily persuaded by the lure of doing *Call of the Wild* (1935) because he admired and had often reread Jack London's novel.

Gable also liked William A. Wellman, the director assigned to the film, but something went sour between them during the shooting, especially when Wellman publicly chided Gable on the set for some unspecified misbehavior. The picture was finished in open animosity and, despite rumors of a romance with co-star Loretta Young, their on-screen communication was as frigid as the snow-covered landscape.

The plot of the novel had been

*AFTER OFFICE HOURS (1935). With Constance Bennett and Harvey Stephens*

CALL OF THE WILD (1935). With Jack Oakie (at left)

distorted in the screenplay by Gene Fowler and Leonard Praskins. Buck, the loyal dog, was no longer the center of the action, now occupied by the Gable-Young star team. There were heavy doses of saccharine dialogue and reviewer André Sennwald in the *New York Times* claimed to have forgotten whether it was Gable or Young who said such lines as "I'll be seeing you every day, every hour, every minute." Sennwald also pointed out that Gable's best scenes were those with the furry Saint Bernard, because the actor was able to change the moonstruck expression he was forced to adopt while gazing at Miss Young.

After *Call of the Wild,* Gable was immediately cast with Jean Harlow in *China Seas* (1935). Tay Garnett, an unjustly forgotten thirties director, moved his agile camera as if on roller skates, stalking the all-star cast all over a ship in peril. The delightfully foolish plot has Harlow, as tarnished and as aspiringly bourgeois as ever, in a blind fury at Gable, who puts her down and prefers satiny Rosalind Russell. Harlow is angry enough to side with villain Wallace Beery, but only until she finds out that he is in league with Malaysian pirates. Reckless but not lawless, Harlow tries to warn Gable, who spurns her and lives to regret it.

*China Seas* has the madly adventurous comic strip air of a "Terry and the Pirates," with Harlow as a Dragon Lady with a heart of gold—or at least of jade. It is still enjoyable to watch and in 1935 it deservedly packed in audiences all over the world. The film now shows more than a passing resemblance to James Bond thrillers of the sixties and Gable fighting against the sadistic Asiatics is an ancestor of the Sean Connery style of heroics.

By then Gable, having won the Academy Award for *It Happened One Night,* was in a position to demand better roles, but he was wary of the challenge when a truly good one came his way. Frank Lloyd, a much-respected director who had won Oscars in 1928 for *The Divine Lady* and in 1932 for *Cavalcade,* had approached Metro with a golden property he had acquired

CHINA SEAS (1935). With Wallace Beery and Jean Harlow

*MUTINY ON THE BOUNTY (1935). With Charles Laughton*

the rights to: Nordhoff and Hall's *Mutiny on the Bounty* trilogy.

Charles Laughton thought Lloyd was a more effective director with props and objects than with actors and feared that the real star of *Mutiny on the Bounty* (1935) would be the ship itself. Gable thought that the star would be Laughton, once he sank his teeth into the succulently villainous part of Captain Bligh. Gable also doubted his own ability to imitate the British accent required by the role of Fletcher Christian and felt he would look ridiculous in pigtail and knee breeches.

The shooting went on and on, way over schedule. More than ever before in his career, Gable was seized by the fear—so effectively instilled by his father— that he would end up looking like "a painted pretty boy."

*MUTINY ON THE BOUNTY (1935). With Movita and Franchot Tone*

Usually patient and jovial on the set, he got panicky and even made a scene when the make-up man tried to apply a powder puff to his shiny nose.

He need not have worried, for Fletcher Christian proved to be one of his most virile parts and it won him enthusiastic praise, as well as a second Academy Award nomination. Laughton and Franchot Tone were also nominated, but they all lost, inexplicably, to the tormented mugging of Victor McLaglen in John Ford's *The Informer. Mutiny on the Bounty* won the Oscar for the best film and was the top box-office attraction of 1935.

In 1962, when MGM tried to repeat its triumph with Marlon Brando, the difference between the two stars became apparent. Brando's neurotic Fletcher Christian had each and every weakness that Gable had avoided. There was not a touch of foppishness in Gable's performance and it smoothly melded integrity with a dash of rascality. It was an affirmation of free spirit and studios tried to copy the style of *Mutiny on the Bounty,* especially Warners with Errol Flynn's dashing but essentially lightweight bouts as a swashbuckler in *Captain Blood* and *The Sea Hawk.*

Gable had pleased his male audiences with *Mutiny on the Bounty* and in his next film he was given back to the ladies. In *Wife vs. Secretary* (1936), director Clarence Brown valiantly jumped into high comedy from the creaky trampoline of a Faith Baldwin novel, *The Office Wife.* The whole enterprise was in constant danger of being unmasked for what it was: a poor man's Noel Coward filigree. The film survives—lamely but surely—on the resiliency of its players: Gable, Harlow, Loy, and James Stewart.

Gable plays a magazine publisher madly in love with wife Myrna Loy. He only has eyes for her and overlooks Harlow, the smart secretary who secretly loves him and functions as the scheming power behind him. James Stewart rounds out the quartet as the gangling suitor who loves Harlow but realizes she is platonically crazy about her boss.

May Robson, as Gable's mother, is the fly in this very sticky ointment. She makes Loy suspicious of Gable's relationship with Harlow. Suddenly jealous and inquisitive, Loy makes Gable take notice of the girl. Meanwhile, Harlow is sagely advising Gable on the intricacies of a magazine merger in the works. When she accidentally discovers that the deal is about to collapse, she flies to Havana where Gable is attending a convention. She warns him of every danger and then supervises a marathon typing session of newly drafted documents.

The following scene annoyed *New York Times* critic Frank Nugent into writing that Gable's forte would never be coyness. Yet Gable has no option but to be coy as he lies exhausted in bed, in that sultry hotel room, right after he and Harlow have been working until two in the morning. She tenderly takes off his shoes and tropical sex floats in to the strains of "Siboney."

The temptation is strong but fleeting. They recover immediately and seem chastely content with sharing nothing more sinful than club sandwiches and coffee. It is Gable's bad luck that at that moment the telephone rings

*WIFE VS. SECRETARY (1936). With (left to right) Jean Harlow, May Robson, Myrna Loy*

and Harlow picks it up in secretarial zeal. It is Myrna Loy, calling long distance from New York, partly because she is lonely and partly to check up on him.

The stigma of adultery is all over the innocent pair and Loy, like any self-respecting wife in a thirties movie, leaves Gable on the spot. Harlow is ready to pick up the pieces and fly with him to Bermuda but she realizes that Gable is only using her to forget Loy, so she personally pleads with the wife to take him back. Defeated but radiantly proud of herself, Harlow goes back to her old steady Stewart.

The film was enormously popular and even after applying every standard of skepticism it is easy to see why. Director Clarence Brown's savoir faire, the gleaming white Cedric Gibbons sets, the shimmering wardrobe—all of it is mildly intoxicating even now. In 1936 it must have been irresistible. So was Gable in impeccably tailored suits, though it is disquieting to hear him throw away a line that indirectly explains his predicament as an actor in this glossy soap opera: "If you want to keep a man honest, never call him a liar."

In *Wife vs. Secretary* it was

SAN FRANCISCO (1936). With Jeanette MacDonald and
Spencer Tracy

his job to convince legions of women fans that he had become the perfect husband required by Loy, Hollywood's perfect wife. He goes through the film like a sexual Mr. Magoo who is totally unaware of his enormous attraction to women. Loy, Harlow, and even May Robson conspire to keep his sex appeal a secret from him. He is faithful, steadfast, and so decent that he gets furious at the suggestion that he should fire a hard-working girl like Harlow just because she's pretty enough to create gossip.

Gable's conversion into domesticity did not last long at MGM and in *San Francisco* (1936) he was cast as Blackie Norton, a cabaret owner in the Barbary Coast who is mean, sexy, and very hard to tame. Jeanette MacDonald comes into his Paradise nightclub looking for a job as a singer and he sub-

SAN FRANCISCO (1936). The famous earthquake sequence

mits her to the indignity of showing her legs, topped by a realistic verdict: "You are a little thin down there but you have a fair set of pipes."

Jeanette MacDonald, MGM's pet canary, had been next in the line of ladies asking to co-star with Gable. He feared her warbling would make the film into another *Dancing Lady* type of musical, with him scowling in the sidewings. Miss MacDonald

later complained that he had looked through her as if she were invisible, but that must have happened on the set. On screen he pays constant attention to her, especially when she makes it coyly clear that she is a virgin. After his first unsuccessful attempt at seduction, he lets her sleep in his apartment because her house has burned down. Acting like a gentleman and regretting it, he draws the curtains to

73

leave her in peace and smiles at the mirror, saying "Good night, sucker."

The Gable-MacDonald team is pallid. *San Francisco* is far more interesting as the first Gable-Tracy film. Throughout their careers and their lives, both men followed a strange pattern of not meeting head on but at odd angles. Gable had one of his first stage triumphs in a part Tracy had originated in *The Last Mile.* For a decade they were the top male stars at MGM and they lunched every day, in hallowed ritual, at the same table in the studio commissary. They were always somewhere in between competitive companions and friendly enemies.

Gable envied Tracy's expressive deadpan, which let feelings glow beneath a restrained exterior. To get a similar effect, Gable sometimes had to contract his features and sweat out an emotion. It was a difference in projection of personality: Tracy was an introvert and Gable an extrovert, but the latter felt the less accomplished for it. On the other hand, Tracy envied Gable for the sex appeal and animal magnetism he lacked.

Tracy was wary of doing *San Francisco* where Gable had the allure, MacDonald had the arias, and he was cramped into a third niche barely above that of a strong supporting player. He and Gable played the traditional tandem of friends: one good, one bad. Director W. S. Van Dyke even included a close-up of a picture of the characters as youngsters: it was a collage made by pasting the adolescent faces of Gable and Tracy on an old photograph.

In *San Francisco,* Gable is Blackie, the shady character, and Tracy is Father Tim. Despite Blackie's godlessness, he has given the priest a four-thousand-dollar organ for his church. Father Tim tells Mary, the Jeanette MacDonald character, that there's more good than bad in Blackie-Gable. He sadly intimates he has not been able to convert him and commissions her for the worthy deed. It works out the other way around when Gable gazes into her eyes and dazzles her by saying, "I love to look at those big lamps of yours." Mesmerized, she gives up singing *Faust* at the opera house to come back and sing ditties in Blackie's joint.

Tracy comes into the club like the wrath of God, berating Gable for letting his fiancée appear in Can Can costume. Gable punches Tracy, who achieves a superbly martyred look as blood trickles down his chin. Mac-

Donald haughtily leaves with Tracy and becomes engaged to an aristocrat, Jack Holt. But it is clear that the unseen star of *San Francisco* is Gable's disputed soul.

Despite the joint efforts of Tracy and MacDonald, Gable can only be saved by the intervention of the mad forces of nature, in the magnificently recreated 1906 earthquake. Fire and brimstone rain upon the wicked city in a visualization of a fervent Louis B. Mayer sermon. When Gable finds MacDonald alive amidst the holocaust, he sinks to his knees and Tracy instructs him to address the deity as naturally as possible. "Thank you, God," Gable exclaims and then, because he was such a deceptive actor, he is given a close-up to say, "I really mean it." Only a historical disaster—plus the awesomely efficient MGM special effects department—could bring him into the fold.

Despite the complaints of the starring trio, *San Francisco* is an exciting film and it was a triumph for everyone involved. The cloth had prevented Tracy from even remotely vying with Gable on a romantic level and he had resented it, but he won the match in the long run. It was Tracy, in a relatively small part,

who was nominated for an Academy Award, while Gable only won MacDonald, a prize doll he didn't want in the first place.

*San Francisco* was followed by four disappointing Gable films. In 1936 W. R. Hearst had moved his Cosmopolitan Pictures to Warners, angry because Irving Thalberg had bypassed Marion Davies and cast Norma Shearer as *Marie Antoinette*. Then, in Hearst's reverie, Miss Davies became the crowning jewel of a Ziegfeldian extravaganza: so *Cain and Mabel* was conceived.

The film was directed by Lloyd Bacon of *42nd Street* fame and the musical numbers were staged by Bobby Connolly, first an assistant and then a rival of Busby Berkeley in the creation of opulent musical numbers. Some very lavish ones were designed for Davies. As Madame du Barry and Lady Guinevere, she ambled around white sets that look like solidified gobs of meringue. *Cain and Mabel* can be described as the apotheosis of "camp," a genre Gable was allergic to.

The plot, such as it is, has Gable as a boxer and Davies as a musical comedy star. She is performing to empty theatres and he in half-filled arenas, so a publicity romance is dreamed up to help them both at the box office.

*CAIN AND MABEL (1936). With (left to right) William Collier Sr., Marion Davies, Allen Jenkins*

They meet in a "cute" manner borrowed from a Rogers-Astaire film, when her tap dancing keeps him awake in a hotel room. They hate each other on sight and Gable debunks Davies' atrocious performances by saying "If the galloping you do is dancing, I've seen better ballet in a horse show."

Davies is infuriated and slaps him. He counters by crowning her with a bucketful of ice cubes. When they meet again, he starts the offensive anew. "If you're a dancer I'm all wet," he growls. She makes his words come true by drenching him with a pitcher of water. It is pure love Hollywood style and Gable succumbs when she offers him a pork chop and he drops the plate on the floor the better to grab her. Later, in an extraordinarily sensual touch, he even licks his lips before he kisses Davies between stacks in a library.

*Cain and Mabel* is an occasionally amusing film because the Laird Doyle screenplay has hilariously acerbic lines for the wonderful supporting players:

Walter Catlett, Ruth Donnelly, Roscoe Karns, and Allen Jenkins. For Gable, it offered next to nothing, but he had to accept it. In 1936, no one antagonized Hearst and Davies without risking ostracism or character assassination in his communications empire.

*Love on the Run* (1936) is another "runaway heiress" comedy with Gable and Crawford in a trans-European chase by plane, train, and ox-cart. John Lee Mahin—in collaboration with Manuel Seff and Gladys Hurlbut—fashioned a screenplay that reworked elements of other Gable successes. The fugitive pair of *It Happened One Night* was moved to France and instead of stopping at a motel they invaded Fontainebleau Palace, where a daffy caretaker (Donald Meek) mistook them for the ghosts of Louis XIV and Madame de Maintenon in the movie's funniest sequence.

*LOVE ON THE RUN (1936). With Donald Meek and Joan Crawford*

*LOVE ON THE RUN (1936). With Joan Crawford*

*PARNELL (1937). With Myrna Loy and (reflected in mirror, left to right) Billie Burke, Alan Marshal, Edna May Oliver*

Franchot Tone played the third man part Robert Montgomery had enacted in *Forsaking All Others* and an adventurous twist was added with Reginald Owen as a menacing spy. Gable was efficient and the film had its moments, but *It Happened One Night* cast its shadow over *Love on the Run.* W. S. Van Dyke was no Capra and Crawford was anything but a stylish comedienne in the manner of Claudette Colbert. The picture suffered accordingly.

In the late thirties and early forties, casting a star as a historical figure was a mark of importance. Muni was Pasteur, Zola, and Juarez, Tracy was Edison, and, in homage to Gable, MGM acquired *Parnell* for him. It had been a Broadway hit play by Elsie T. Schauffler dealing with the ill-fated love of the Irish Nationalist leader for a married woman, Katie O'Shea. John Van Druten and S. N. Behrman wrote the screenplay and a serious, academic director like John Stahl was chosen. The impressive supporting cast included Edmund Gwenn, Edna May

Oliver, Alan Marshal, and Donald Crisp.

*Parnell* (1937) was every inch a prestige picture, redolent of wax museum stuffiness. Even obedient Joan Crawford had sense enough to plead with Mayer to escape playing Katie, a role Myrna Loy had the misfortune to inherit. Gable was initially pleased with doing this respectable vehicle, but he grew to hate the film so vehemently that after he married Carole Lombard she used to taunt him—in his rare moments of arrogance— by merely whispering, "Remember *Parnell.*"

The film has acquired a reputation as a total disaster mainly because it was the rare Gable movie that lost money, and a red mark in the MGM books was the equivalent of a scarlet letter. It is a self-important and dull picture, but by no means a disgrace. Parnell is historically described as frail, nervous, haughty, and sensitive, so obviously Gable was miscast, but he was sensible enough not to try for a characterization along these impossible lines. He played Gable: it was not accurate, but it was not embarrassing.

He was back on safer ground with Harlow in *Saratoga* (1937). She had given a surprisingly adroit performance in *Wife vs. Secretary* in a subdued role with not a trace of her trademarked vulgarity. Just before her death, she was upgraded in the MGM scale of leading ladies and in *Saratoga* she even turned "uppity" as an American girl who comes back from England to run her father's racing stables. She attempts a hoity-toity British accent and has a dull, rich fiancé in tow (Walter Pidgeon).

Gable again plays a disreputable guy. As a racetrack bookmaker, he wants Harlow for himself, but sees nothing wrong in her stringing Pidgeon along, since they both need a "chump" to finance his schemes. Harlow correctly diagnoses his attitude as a kind of pimping, not unlike what had taken place during that first sleazy half hour of *Hold Your Man.* She is properly indignant and tells Gable so. His character has such a woozy sense of values that his reaction is bafflement. He can't for the life of him see what she is talking about.

It is impossible to tell what *Saratoga* had in store for its stars, since it is disjointed and clearly incomplete. Harlow died before finishing it and MGM considered shelving the project, but then the screenplay was hastily rewritten and Mary

*SARATOGA (1937). With Jean Harlow*

Dees, Harlow's double, completed a few scenes. *Saratoga* was rushed into theatres less than two months after Harlow's death. Filmgoers were lured by morbid curiosity and by the macabre game of spotting, scene by scene, who was Harlow and who was Mary Dees. The picture was one of the top moneymakers of 1937, but it stands as a depressing conclusion to one of the gayest movie partnerships in film history.

Another (and very different) screen partnership turned up again in *Test Pilot* (1938), where Gable becomes the quizzical Quixote to Tracy's ponderous Panza. Gable is a daredevil aviator who pushes planes and himself to the limits of endurance. Tracy is Gable's mechanic: practical, soothing, and restrictive. Like a dutiful mother, he urges Gable to stay off the booze and get all the sleep he can. In the very first scene, Gable walks into a hotel room with an acquiescent broad, but Tracy brusquely

*TEST PILOT (1938). With Myrna Loy and Spencer Tracy*

takes her away so that Gable can get his rest for next morning's ordeal.

As a test pilot, Gable is doomed to prove his manhood over and over again. He has barely survived so many times that he is speeding through life with the recklessness of those living on borrowed time. When he is grounded at Myrna Loy's Kansas farm, he is fuming at having come short of breaking the coast-to-coast record. Yet he is immediately attracted to this bright, pretty girl and he is impressed by her diploma from State University. (He admits that he broke another record by "starting school as a sophomore and ending up as a freshman.")

Gable tries to fight the attraction, but he is hooked forever when they go to a baseball game and she outdoes everyone in shouting and calling the plays. Here, at last, is a girl with some brains who can also be a pal. He courts her and, though she tries to make him jealous with a proper boy friend in Kansas, he talks her into a spur-of-the-moment marriage. He brings her back to his all-male family, made up of boss Lionel Barrymore and mechanic Tracy.

Tracy is initially distrustful of Loy, but he soon mellows into calling her "pal," just like her husband of several hours. He even helps them buy Loy a nightgown for their wedding night. This highly charged three-way relationship ascends to dizzying heights of innocence when both Tracy and Loy watch Gable risking his life up in the clouds. During the Cleveland aerial races, Gable's motor briefly catches fire and Loy panics, but Tracy reassures her by saying, almost in a trance of concerned admiration: "Don't worry, he doesn't mind a little fire; he's asbestos."

Gable escapes death and Loy suddenly realizes, looking at Tracy's tear-streaked face, how much he too loves Gable and how hard the years of sending him to a probable death must have been for this man. In a gesture of the purest tenderness, Loy kisses Tracy, murmuring, "God bless you, Gunner." In his best "Aw, shucks" manner, he replies: "It's all right, pal."

*Test Pilot* gets down to business with its aerial scenes, the crowd pleasers that made the film very profitable. Finally Tracy is crushed to death by excess weight in an overloaded test plane. A story made the rounds in Hollywood that Tracy was so annoyed with his part that he stretched this scene as far as he could, to get some extra footage of his own, while Gable laughingly protested between take after take of Tracy's agony: "Die, Spence, for Pete's sake." Tracy was insuring himself with a "good moment." He was shrewd enough to assess the danger to his star personality in playing the kind of amiable capon role he was given in *Test Pilot*.

Regrets were unnecessary since both men, under Victor Fleming's direction, are superb in the film. Tracy munches his chewing gum as if his life depended on it and then presses the wad, for good luck, on the fuselage of Gable's plane. And Gable is not to be upstaged: he is at the top of his animal gracefulness and is described by Loy as "a bear who turns his head to gaze, undecided whether to jump on you or not," and later as "a cross between an Indian and a gazelle."

The memorable scenes, of course, are the ones with Tracy. Both were so unimpeachably masculine that they could embody the sweetest male camaraderie without a shadow of homoerotic innuendo. Gable playfully embraces Tracy, saying, "I love you, Gunner." After his beloved pal has been long dead and Gable has renounced test piloting to become an Air Corps instructor, he still remembers Tracy in a poignant gesture: he places a wad of gum on the fuselage of another pilot's plane, just as Gunner used to do with him.

MGM breathed down Tracy's neck several times to repeat the Gable-Tracy team in the late thirties, but he kept insisting he would rather go on suspension. Around this time, Tracy drove into the lot one day to see Gable besieged by autograph hunters. As he parted the crowd with the fenders of his slowly moving car, he shouted at Gable: "Hail the King." The joke was carried further when Tracy had a crown made out of cardboard and then placed it on Gable's head during a mock ceremony at their special table in the Metro dining room, thus proclaiming him King of the Lot.

Ed Sullivan heard the story and promptly organized a nationwide contest to choose the King and Queen of Hollywood. To no one's surprise Gable was elected King, with Myrna Loy riding his ermine coattails as Queen. They were officially proclaimed in Sullivan's radio show. This publicity stunt had lasting consequences and until his death Gable was known as the King. It was Tracy's joke that put him on the throne.

Gable and Loy, the King and his Queen, immediately went into *Too Hot to Handle* (1938), a trivial comedy-melodrama directed by Jack Conway in a speedy manner that gave audiences no time to recognize the Gable character as a monster in charming disguise. He had by far his most cynical role as the newsreel reporter who stopped at nothing to find or invent a highly photographic event.

Gable goes as far as to hide his cameras in an ambulance and chase the plane Myrna Loy is piloting, forcing her to an emergency landing on the other side of the field, where the competition can't get all the close-up footage. The plane crashes and burns, but Gable rescues Loy and she falls in love with him. The reviewers were appalled at his methods, but the audience was as permissive as Loy: nothing Gable did was too hot for his fans to handle.

It was 1939 and Gable was well into his stride as a great star when *Idiot's Delight* came

*TOO HOT TO HANDLE (1938). As newsreel cameraman Chris Hunter*

*IDIOT'S DELIGHT (1939). With Norma Shearer and Fritz Feld*

his way. MGM had bought Robert E. Sherwood's acclaimed play about a fake Russian countess and the hoofer who was once her lover. They meet at a Swiss hotel on the eve of a world war and stage a crafty duel between his earthiness and her delusions. Alfred Lunt and Lynn Fontanne had originated the roles on Broadway, and though the film version moved the pacifist theme into the background, it was nonetheless prophetic. It was released in January 1939, and hostilities started in Europe seven months later.

In *Idiot's Delight,* Gable is in top form. The eyebrows have become independently mobile and operate as restless circumflex accents, rising higher and higher as Shearer escalates her outrageous repertory of lies. She is also perfect for a part that absorbs every mannerism, making the Shearer fakery no longer a curse but a blessing.

When she describes her incredible escapes from the Soviets, Gable knows all too well she is the same vaudeville aerialist he casually bedded years before in Omaha. She is undaunted by his disbelief and purrs: "You say I met you in Omaha . . . Oma . . .

ha. . . . Is that in Persia?" His face rearranges itself into a poem of half-irate, half-admiring incredulity as he watches her act.

Through most of the film, he plays the role with tongue-in-cheek cynicism. He does a superb parody of third-rate hoofing with a sextet called "Harry's Girls." He punctures Charles Coburn's pomposity by genially saying: "Don't apologize. I've been rude to many people and never regretted it." He mocks the menacing militarism of Joseph Schildkraut's totalitarian villain and even flattens the tiresome and ineffectual eagerness of pacifist Burgess Meredith by benignly smiling at him while growling: "Hurry on, you got no time to lose, you gotta save the world."

Yet it is pragmatic Gable who at the last moment forsakes his iron practicality to come back to save Shearer from the incoming brutes. When he fails, he is equally willing to die with her. The Sherwood play ended with an intimation of death by a bombing holocaust, as the leads laughed and sang on the verge of being blown to bits. The film version, as directed by Clarence Brown, has one of those tacked-on happy endings that were a special feature of MGM movies, and there is a vision of hope as the planes rumble away while Gable and Shearer, miraculously intact, join voices in a church hymn.

The great challenge was next: with *Gone with the Wind* (1939), Gable faced the moment of truth. He was so perfect for the part of Rhett Butler that it is surprising to discover how close he came to never playing it. There were many detours on his long, ascending way to Tara.

During a four-day coast-to-coast train ride, Mervyn LeRoy's wife read the Margaret Mitchell novel, still in galleys. She urged him to secure the screen rights as a vehicle for Miriam Hopkins and Gable—if Warners could pry him away from MGM. LeRoy refused to even read the book, insisting that there was no money in Civil War pictures.

LeRoy's wife had immediately cast Gable as Rhett, but David O. Selznick did not, for reasons of his own. Selznick had left his highly regarded position as a producer at Metro, fleeing the tyranny of Louis B. Mayer, then his father-in-law. The parting had not been amicable and Selznick knew Mayer would never let him have Gable without some MGM strings attached.

Selznick had bought the book for fifty thousand dollars, a record sum at that time. He so

GONE WITH THE WIND (1939).
As Rhett Butler

loathed the idea of doing business with his old family studio that he risked miscasting the role of Rhett Butler just to escape the Mayer trap. He considered Gary Cooper and even started negotiations at Warners to borrow Bette Davis for Scarlett O'Hara and Errol Flynn for Rhett: the plan was scuttled by Davis' adamant refusal to co-star with Flynn.

It was useless to run away from Gable, because the novel had become the biggest best seller in publishing memory and the readers had cast him in their minds as Rhett Butler. No one else would do. Selznick faced the inevitable and went to Mayer, who said he would only lend Gable if the film were distributed by his company, Loew's Incorporated.

Gable had been regarded as a willing commodity by one and all. To their great shock, they found out he had not read the book and claimed to have no idea what they were talking about. He raced through the novel during a nerve-racking weekend and came back with his astounding verdict: Rhett was a Ronald Colman role and he had no desire or intention to play it.

Luckily, there was another matter to be taken into account. Though Gable had no use for

Rhett, he certainly could use money: he had fallen in love with Carole Lombard and his estranged wife, Rhea Langham, would not give him a divorce unless she received a cash settlement of over a quarter of a million dollars. Mayer knew that Gable was afraid the price of freedom would clean him out, since there were rumors that Langham was changing lawyers and might raise the ante. Mayer cajoled his star with a hundred-thousand-dollar bonus and Gable accepted the film. He had been corraled into it by his private predicament and by the millions of fans who thought he was the prototype for Rhett.

Their casting was easy to understand. It is impossible to read about Butler's lopsided grin and impudent manner without automatically arriving at the Gable image. Selznick needed Gable and the film was delayed for a year because the star was otherwise committed. This hiatus was employed in creating publicity suspense around the search for an actress to play Scarlett, but the game went on too long and when Gable was finally ready there was still no co-star.

Vivien Leigh won the role in a last-minute decision over director George Cukor's judgment. He had wanted Katharine Hepburn, but was soon impressed by Leigh's talent. They became fast friends and allies, multiplying Gable's misgivings from the starting date on. Vivien Leigh always had a tendency to soften her characters and make them more sympathetic than the author intended—e.g., her magnificent but slightly sweetened Blanche in Elia Kazan's *A Streetcar Named Desire.*

Leigh judged Scarlett "a terrible bitch" and contrived to whitewash her around the edges, with Cukor's complicity. Gable sounded the alarm and Cukor was replaced by Victor Fleming, a director Gable trusted. Leigh and Olivia de Havilland dressed in widow's weeds from the wardrobe department and staged a sobbing sit-in to make Selznick reinstate Cukor, but to no avail. At this point, Gable was the one indispensable player.

It all worked out well for *Gone with the Wind,* in one of those off-camera miracles that sometimes shape memorable movies. At night and on the sly, Cukor began coaching Leigh and de Havilland, while Gable had the steadying influence of Fleming on the set. In this tug of war something had to give and it was Fleming's nerves. Harassed by the rebellious Leigh, he collapsed on the set and was hospitalized. Sam Wood, another Gable-approved director, took *Gone with the Wind* in hand. He had a knack as an organizer and put the Cukor and Fleming influences into proper perspective.

The film was an unending ordeal for Gable. He was often wary of the demands of the role and his insecurity reached its low point when he was forced to break down and cry on screen. Once before in his film career he had been on the verge of tears, in the last scene of *Hold Your Man*. It had turned out disastrously and he refused to repeat the experience. He took refuge in Olivia de Havilland's dressing room and for hours she persuaded him to give it at least a try. When he finally faced the cameras he was so wrought up that it took only one take to achieve one of the finest moments of his career.

Fleming had recovered and when he came back the situation was very awkward. There were days when Fleming worked in the morning and Wood in the afternoon, but all in all *Gone with the Wind* is Fleming's film. His credit as director—sometimes argued over by purists—is indisputable. Watching his work with Gable in *Red Dust* and *Test Pilot* offers enough assurance that Fleming's was the dominant style in *Gone with the Wind*.

As always, Fleming took very good care of Gable and Rhett is the actor's ideal character. From the moment he watches Scarlett come down the stairs at Twelve Oaks, he is more than undressing her with his sharp eyes; he is X-raying her character down to the last pretension of grandeur. Scarlett O'Hara, as tartly played by Vivien Leigh, is the ultimate challenge for the Gable man, because she is his female counterpart.

Scarlett-Leigh does everything Gable had excelled at in previous roles. She prefers the wan gentleman Leslie Howard embodies as Ashley Wilkes, exactly as Gable had favored Mary Astor and Rosalind Russell over Harlow in *Red Dust* and *China Seas*. Scarlett is the tough woman attracted by the weak man who eludes her. Captain Butler poses a threat and she feigns to despise him because she deeply fears him.

It takes Scarlett-Leigh the whole of the Civil War, ante and post bellum, to come to terms with her dilemma as the hunted huntress. Gable-Rhett waits, with his mind focused on her, but never succumbing to the exclusive obsession of taming this shrew.

GONE WITH THE WIND (1939). With Leslie Howard

GONE WITH THE WIND (1939). With Hattie McDaniel

GONE WITH THE WIND (1939). With Vivien Leigh

GONE WITH THE WIND (1939). With (left to right) Olivia de Havilland, Ward Bond, Leslie Howard

All through *Gone with the Wind,* Gable is free to be platonically coquettish and deferential with Melanie (Olivia de Havilland), the virtuous woman he admires. He flirts outrageously with Mammy (Hattie McDaniel) and wins her over to his camp with the gift of a red taffeta skirt. He is sweet and fatherly with his doomed daughter Bonnie (Cammie King) and completely relaxed with the whore Belle Watling (Ona Munson), with whom he suggests the gentle camaraderie of weary bedfellows. It is like an entire harem of female types he had contended with in his film career, and he plays sultan among them with a flair.

Only Scarlett, in her pursuit of Ashley, eludes Captain Butler. When she finally has Ashley within her grasp, she realizes the hollowness of her stubborn quest. She wanders, lost in the fog, living the nightmare that has haunted her throughout the film. At the end of the bad dream, there is reality. In a flash, she discovers Rhett Butler has always been the only man for her. But it is much too late for both of them.

When Scarlett admits she loved him all along, he wearily says: "Frankly, my dear, I don't give a damn." He walks out on her, and that slamming door is as final as the one Ibsen's Nora closes at the end of *A Doll's House.* The play has been hailed as a harbinger of woman's liberation and Rhett's last words in *Gone with the Wind* equally state a credo of male liberation in the Gable manner.

Both novel and film are shrewdly open-ended. Scarlett has hopes that she will lure Rhett back and that "After all, tomorrow is another day." But she is all alone, on the hill overlooking Tara, in that last unforgettable shot. Will Rhett come back to her or is he gone forever? The continuing appeal of *Gone with the Wind* derives to no small degree from the fact that both men and women can leave the theatre with opposite and similarly satisfying answers to that question.

From the day it opened, *Gone with the Wind* was a phenomenon. It made more money than any other film in history and it won an unprecedented ten Academy Awards. Gable was nominated but lost, according to one of those unconfirmable stories about Oscar shenanigans, because Mayer ordered the powerful Metro block vote to side with Robert Donat in *Goodbye, Mr. Chips,* a home lot movie that needed more help at the

93

box office than the fabulous *Gone with the Wind.*

*GWTW,* the only film to be identified by its initials, has been revived many times, never losing its strength and climbing to new records every time around. It placed Gable, King of Hollywood, at the very peak. It was a dangerous spot to be in. How could he top *GWTW?*

Gable did not even try. He was too happy in his personal life to bother. He had married Carole Lombard on March 29, 1939, and had taken her, arm in arm, as his reigning Queen, to the now legendary Atlanta premiere of *Gone with the Wind* on December 15 of that year. In his ranch at Encino, he achieved such peace and contentment with her that he seriously started talking of retiring permanently as soon as his MGM contract expired.

Subsequent films were not as good as *Gone with the Wind* but he didn't mind much. That would have been trying for the impossible and he was never a rainbow chaser, either as an actor or a man. There were rewards for his practicality, such as *Strange Cargo* (1940), the best of his dramas with Joan Crawford. Under Frank Borzage's direction, she was excellent as a defeated, cynical

prostitute and Gable was equally good as the leader of a group of convicts escaping from a penal colony in New Guinea.

The salvation of renegade Gable's soul was a recurrent theme in his MGM movies—e.g., *San Francisco* and *Adventure.* It was poetically stated in *Strange Cargo,* where Ian Hunter plays a mysterious Christlike figure who joins the fugitives and leads them to repentance, one by one. The strong supporting cast included Paul Lukas, Peter Lorre, Albert Dekker and Eduardo Ciannelli. The film was not merely another try at MGM religiosity: in Frank Borzage's sensitive hands, the allegory of Good vs. Evil, though highly fanciful, was never ludicrous. Even the brutish Gable character managed a persuasive transition at the end, when he voluntarily returned to serve his sentence and pay for his sins.

In 1940, Tracy could no longer hold out against playing Gable's patient pal and they were co-starred in *Boom Town.* Just the names of the characters hint at how MGM had cast them as the modern Quixote and Panza: Gable plays "Big John" and Tracy is "Square John." They start as partners in wildcat oil drilling. Gable womanizes and Tracy dreams of marrying the

*STRANGE CARGO (1940). With Ian Hunter and Joan Crawford*

girl he left back home (Claudette Colbert).

When Colbert appears on the scene, she falls for Gable instead. They get married, Tracy forgives and forgets, and quickly becomes Third Musketeer to Gable and Colbert, just as he had to Gable and Loy in *Test Pilot*. As in *San Francisco*, Tracy is also Gable's puritanical Jiminy Cricket and in his role as nagging conscience he breaks the business partnership when he suspects Gable of being unfaithful to Colbert. They gamble for the whole enterprise, Gable loses and leaves, penniless, with long-suffering Colbert.

Years later their paths recross. Gable is having an affair with Hedy Lamarr and it is now Tracy's turn to lose all his money in an effort to bring his errant friend back to Colbert. Further complications are contrived to ruin them both again, because John Lee Mahin's

*BOOM TOWN (1940). With Hedy Lamarr*

96

COMRADE X (1940). With Hedy Lamarr

screenplay has a queer nostalgia for bankruptcy. In the last shot, all three are walking arm in arm to a new, undrilled field, starting from scratch but happy in the regained togetherness of a platonic *ménage-à-trois*.

Gable enjoyed making *Boom Town* because it brought back memories of his early days in the oil fields. He got along well with director Jack Conway and they played constant practical jokes on each other. With Colbert, it was a pleasant reunion after their joint triumph in *It Happened One Night*. Tracy detested his part and the film. He vowed never again to play the restrictive Duenna to Gable's Don Juan, and *Boom Town* was their last appearance as a team.

*Comrade X* (1940) tried to re-create the magic of *Ninotchka* with mistaken ingredients. The farcical screenplay by Ben Hecht and Charles Lederer has Gable, an American reporter in Russia, in an initially unpromising relationship with a trolley conductor

97

*THEY MET IN BOMBAY (1941). With Rosalind Russell*

(Hedy Lamarr). She is such a staunch Communist that the Moscow government, in disbelief of her zeal, is having her investigated.

King Vidor, a fine director in his own right, was all wrong for this kind of material and the film degenerated into some heavy-handed slapstick. Gable was properly dynamic and Lamarr, never a very animated actress, was effective as the frozen-faced fanatic. Nearly everyone who could roll his "r's" in Hollywood was recruited for a cast that included Oscar Homolka, Felix Bressart, Sig Rumann, Mikhail Rasumny and Vladimir Sokoloff. They all tried bravely, but *Comrade X* came alive only fitfully.

*They Met in Bombay* (1941) starts as an amusing comedy about jewel thieves trying to outwit each other. Gable and Rosalind Russell handled the brittle dialogue adroitly under Clarence Brown's smooth direction, but then the drawing-room

*HONKY TONK (1941). With Lana Turner and Albert Dekker*

comedy style detoured abruptly into some very foolish adventures. While posing as a British captain, Gable is unable to avoid being sent to the front, where he bravely fights the Japanese and is decorated with the Victoria Cross for heroism displayed during his imposture. Like so many times in his career, he goes to jail in the end, with the understanding that it won't be for long, making it safe for Rosalind Russell to also reform and wait for him.

*Honky Tonk* (1941) launched the highly bankable combination of Gable and Lana Turner. She was starting her career at MGM just at the point where death had stopped Harlow's. In her last two films with Gable, Harlow had graduated to the level of a sexy but nice leading lady. Turner had similar qualities: she was cute, piquant, but not vulgar. She also was kittenish and it brought out the roving feline in Gable's style.

*Honky Tonk* could have been

*SOMEWHERE I'LL FIND YOU (1942). With Charles Dingle and Robert Sterling*

a far better movie, but the screenplay by Marguerite Roberts and John Sanford goes off in so many tangents that Jack Conway seems to be directing not the movie but the traffic. Gable plays a rascal in a Western town who escapes being tarred and feathered in the first scene and goes on to chisel his way to the top. He has the entire town under his thumb and runs it with the shady elegance of a minor Rhett Butler.

Turner is the well-brought-up daughter of another con man (Frank Morgan). Always ready to leave a tart to pursue a virgin, Gable turns his back on his dancehall girl (Claire Trevor) and marries Turner, to her father's chagrin. From then on the plot is a string of incidents designed to make Gable abandon his wicked ways: Morgan is killed, Turner has a miscarriage and is on the verge of dying. All this melodrama slows down the film,

*With third wife Carole Lombard*

*Gable in the Army Air Corps, World War II*

but *Honky Tonk* is entertaining and proved very popular.

When Gable started his next film with Turner, *Somewhere I'll Find You* (1942), it was a month after Pearl Harbor and he had been named chairman of Hollywood's Victory Committee. He assigned Carole Lombard to go to Indiana and open a bond drive near Fort Wayne, her home town. She sold more than two million dollars in bonds and sent Gable a telegram saying: "Pappy, you'd better join this man's Army."

Anxious to get back to him, she cancelled her train reservations and flew back with her mother and her agent, Otto Winkler. On January 16, 1942, the TWA skyliner crashed head-on into Table Mountain, near Las Vegas. Gable stood an anguished death watch, waiting for a search party to go up the mountain and try to find some sign of life in the wreckage. Spencer Tracy joined him and persuaded him not to go up with the party. They all knew there would be no survivors and they wanted to spare Gable.

He came back to Hollywood, almost crazed with grief. He shut himself up at the Encino ranch and insisted on preserving everything just as Lombard had left it, down to the spilled face powder in front of her mirror. Production stopped for weeks on *Somewhere I'll Find You* and there were rumors it would be definitely shelved.

Gable was too much of a professional and he eventually came back to finish the picture. It was doubly painful because it was directed by Wesley Ruggles, the man who had guided him in *No Man of Her Own*, his only film with Lombard. Gable played a war correspondent whose brother, Robert Sterling, died in action and the screenplay con-

tained painful lines about death and heroism. When Gable heard that some of them were being rewritten to spare him pain, he insisted that they be kept in. He wanted no deference and no pity.

*Somewhere I'll Find You,* conceived as a semicomedy, had unavoidably somber overtones. The critics pointed them out and treated it respectfully but, like *Saratoga,* it was overtaken by events and is one of those films where reality weighs heavily on the fiction. Its box-office success was, again, based on morbid curiosity.

It was Gable's last film for three years. Overage at forty-one, he enlisted in the Air Force. It had been Lombard's last wish in that fateful telegram and he could not dispel his guilt feelings at having sent her on the bond drive. For once, MGM was helpless and had no option but to let the King go.

"**G**able's back and Garson's got him" occupies a special niche among Hollywood's trashiest slogans. In fact, it was worse than merely a come-on for fans who had missed the King for three years. That catch phrase was an omen of what MGM had in store for their conquering hero. To be "had" by Garson in the forties was the equivalent of being shorn by Shearer in the thirties. Shearer had been the boss's wife; Garson was Mayer's impossible dream of antiseptic sex.

Gable had returned from the European front justifiably proud. In 1942, General "Hap" Arnold, head of the Air Force, experienced some trouble getting enlisted men to become gunners in heavy bombers and he commissioned Gable to prepare a film that would make that position more attractive and exciting.

Gable flew as a gunner over occupied France and risked his life many times to get some breathtaking photography on air raids over Germany. John Lee Mahin, who had written the screenplays of several of his films, was then an intelligence officer and Gable prevailed upon him to write a story about two young gunners who would reenact the thrills and hardships of the dangerous missions he actually flew.

# THE POSTWAR AND FINAL YEARS

After eight months on the job, Gable and Mahin came back to Washington, treasuring all that hard-earned footage. "Hap" Arnold then told Gable that his film had been superseded by William Wyler's *The Memphis Belle*. Also about gunners in heavy bombers, Wyler's picture had impressed the Air Force higher echelon and it was set for wide distribution and ultimate acclaim.

Gable's effort ended up as *Combat America*, a 63-minute training film occasionally shown at bond rallies. Some of his aerial photography was also edited into *Wings Up*, a training short for AAF officers where Gable appeared in person: it was little more than a recruiting poster. For once, Gable had worked very hard on something he passionately believed in, but it quickly sank into oblivion. It is difficult to blame him for holding thereafter to his policy of no risks taken.

In 1944, discharged from the Air Force with the rank of major, he again joined Metro. They had a brand new uniform waiting for

*Gable at his ranch before starting ADVENTURE (1945)*

him: respectability was embroidered on both lapels. Greer Garson, the current first lady of the MGM salon, had misgivings about being paired with Gable. She guessed it would not work out well for either of them, but she was thrust against him with forcibly open arms. *Adventure* (1945) was her crucifixion and Gable's apostasy, according to the Mayer gospel.

Mayer wanted Gable's comeback film to be very emotional and heart-tugging. He had even lured William Saroyan to MGM with the promise of letting him direct the film version of his novel, *The Human Comedy.* The author left when he found out that what Mayer really wanted him to work on was an adaptation of Florence Barclay's *The Rosary,* a hopelessly outmoded, soppy, and sentimental novel. Mayer dreamed of it as a vehicle for Gable's reentry into films.

The final choice was *This Strange Adventure,* a novel by Clyde Brion Davis which, unbelievably, MGM had originally acquired for Freddie Bartholomew. In *Adventure,* as it eventually was called, Gable plays a sailor who falls for Garson, a supposedly prim librarian who punches a guy in a bar and has a floozy (Joan Blondell) for a roommate.

MGM had stifled Garson behind the Mrs. Miniver type of iron mask and the screenplay for *Adventure* had four different writers trying to loosen her up. They were only partially effective and her character is contradictory: its still waters run so deep that they could only be successfully explored by Jacques Cousteau.

Gable does not go for Blondell, the Harlow prototype, but for Garson. He marries her and then deserts her to follow his seafaring buddy, wretchedly played by Thomas Mitchell as a cross between Beery and Tracy, marinated in rye. Before he dies, Mitchell unctuously persuades Gable to return to Garson. He comes back just in time to revive their still-born baby by asking God a favor for the first time in his life.

Even more than *Hold Your Man*—which it curiously resembles—*Adventure* is the ultimate Louis B. Mayer mixture of sin, retribution, and redemption by miracle. It is apocalyptically bad, but it made money on its star-crossed marquee value and would be unimportant in Gable's career except that it set the pattern for what was going to happen to him at MGM. From then on, in the postwar years, there

*ADVENTURE (1945). With Greer Garson and Thomas Mitchell*

was a conspiracy afoot to scratch the rough Gable surface, so that the soft core of idealism could be extracted for mass consumption.

Like the thirties tough guys who grew up imitating him, Gable had proved that he was able to shed the hard crust and shine forth in combat. The postwar elevation of Gable's image was more than the scaffolding for a successful film personality: it was almost the underpinning of a platform for any Gable-inspired veteran to run for office on.

Gable enjoyed the part he played in this fantasy. Always unhappy with the disreputable roles he was given in the thirties, he apparently welcomed the change of pace. He initially refused his next film, *The Hucksters* (1947), based on the best-selling Frederick Wakeman novel he blasted as "filthy and not entertainment." Clark Gable in the thirties would have breezed through it; Major Gable in the forties considered it beneath his newly acquired dignity as an ex-combatant.

*THE HUCKSTERS (1947). With Ava Gardner and Edward Arnold*

The Luther Davis screenplay underwent revisions that turned the adulterous heroine into a widow and changed the debunking of Madison Avenue advertising agencies into a satire on radio. *The Hucksters* was not essentially harmed and it is still one of the bright patches in those last murky years at Metro. The refurbished plot has Gable paying scant attention to the Harlow symbol (Ava Gardner) and pursuing ladylike Deborah Kerr, in her first American picture.

To impress idealistic Kerr, he renounces the evil world of hucksterism and becomes a crusader at fade-out. The film is briskly directed by Jack Conway and contains one of Gable's memorable moments, as he dunks a pretentious capitalist (Sydney Greenstreet) with a pitcher of water. It is the equivalent of Gable's rebellion against his boss in *It Happened One Night,* but

*HOMECOMING (1948). With Lana Turner*

funny as it is when remembered out of context, it finally rings hollow as a gesture. From the "new" Gable MGM was trying to promote, it was not an act of faith, but of smugness.

From then on it was decline in a roller coaster and Gable's last years at MGM had few rewards. *Homecoming* (1948) paired him again with Lana Turner and the ads called them "The TEAM that generates STEAM." They were directed by Mervyn LeRoy,

the man who had discovered Turner in *They Won't Forget* and who had tried to give Gable the gigolo part Douglas Fairbanks Jr. eventually played in *The Public Enemy.* Ever since Jack Warner had overruled his decision in that film, LeRoy had wanted to work with Gable, whom he thought "a charismatic actor."

In *Homecoming,* Gable plays the same type of "society doctor" Robert Donat had tried be-

*COMMAND DECISION (1948). As Brigadier General K.C. Dennis*

COMMAND DECISION (1948). With Walter Pidgeon

fore in *The Citadel*. Gable learns the humanistic values during wartime, through a love-hate relationship with Turner. In the thirties, it would have taken him five minutes flat to come to terms with the girl, but they spend three years shadow boxing and yield to temptation only when they meet on leave in Paris, the ultimate procuress of a city in Hollywood lore.

Gable looks remarkably unconcerned as Turner subsequently pays for her sins by dying of injuries received during the Battle of the Bulge. The clue to the picture's place in Gable's mythology is in its original title:

*The Homecoming of Ulysses.* That is the name of the character he plays and Anne Baxter is his wife Penny, short for Penelope. The shrewdly calculated plot reassured every American Penny-Penelope that no matter what her wicked Ulysses might have done during his war years, he could be forgiven and led back to PTA meetings. The New York critics selected *Homecoming* as one of the ten worst movies of 1948, but this corn-flaked "Odyssey" was taken to heart by the ladies and made money for the studio.

*Command Decision* (1948) landed him a good part that was

ANY NUMBER CAN PLAY (1949). At head of table: Frank Morgan

beyond his range. Paul Kelly, a good introspective actor, had created it in the Broadway hit by William Wister Haines. Under Sam Wood's direction, Gable was not as effective as Kelly in conveying the moral agony of a flight commander forced to send his men on near suicidal raids over Germany. Gable tried hard, but he was an extrovert actor in an introvert role. He remained brusque and impatient throughout all the soul-searching and Walter Pidgeon stole the picture as the sort of blithe expert in one-up-manship that Major Gable was considered too heroic to portray.

*Any Number Can Play* (1949) was again directed by Mervyn LeRoy and presents Gable as a stodgy casino owner married to elegant Alexis Smith, in a vision of what the gambler in *Saratoga* and *No Man of Her Own* would have become after steady doses of script-induced morality. Gable is a defanged sharpie, described in the film as "a nut for human dignity." He is even seen sternly pushing a prostitute out

*KEY TO THE CITY (1950). With Loretta Young and James Gleason*

of his establishment.

All this clean living in film after film got its dubious reward in *Key to the City* (1950), in which Major Gable becomes Mayor Gable. At a convention of mayors he meets Loretta Young, also a mayor, and they compromise their political future by briefly going to jail after a silly fracas. Under George Sidney's traditionally permissive direction, Gable desperately makes faces, trying to pump some life into a moribund comedy. It is one of his few embarrassing per-

formances.

Yet, with the exception of *Key to the City,* Gable went through the shorn flock of movies in a series of performances that are never less than interesting, often more than workmanlike, and sometimes brilliant. Ironically, the plots of his films turned against him when he was at his most proficient as an actor.

For instance, when he slapped Barbara Stanwyck in *To Please a Lady* (1950) it was with more style and conviction than when he first struck her, twenty years

*Gable and his fourth wife, Lady Sylvia Ashley*

*TO PLEASE A LADY (1950). With fellow racing drivers*

before in *Night Nurse,* but the movie was a dispirited reworking of *Test Pilot,* with midget auto racing instead of daredevil aviation. Gable had by then absorbed the elements of the Tracy role and needed no sidekick: he was his own dynamo and setback. But under Clarence Brown's curiously indifferent direction, the finesse had become finagling; the double image was perfect but the mirror was broken.

*Across the Wide Missouri* (1951) is of special interest as a truncated film of promise. It is also rich in cross-references to Gable's career. It was directed by William A. Wellman of *Night Nurse* and *Call of the Wild;* the mad trapper is played by Adolphe Menjou, the erstwhile suave seducer of *The Easiest Way,* and Jack Holt, Gable's rival in *San Francisco,* is a venerable if somewhat incongruous Indian chief.

After their disagreement on the set of *Call of the Wild,* Wellman thought Gable would never work with him again, but the

*ACROSS THE WIDE MISSOURI (1951). As trapper Flint Mitchell*

*ACROSS THE WIDE MISSOURI (1951).*

star was delighted, hoping that a solid, professional action director would get him out of his impasse. Wellman surprised everyone by making a plotless, wrong-headed, lyrical Western. The film is an honest try at a quasi-documentary feature on the plight of French and Scottish trappers in Indian territory. Everything is slow and bucolic, with quaint characters lingered on lovingly by the camera. There are memorable bits and pieces, such as a sequence in which a demented Menjou runs around in clanking armor, or another in which a group of trappers sing carols in French on a snowy Christmas night.

In the Gable character, a noble, somewhat defeated, almost valetudinarian profile began to emerge. His marriage to the Indian girl (María Elena Marqués) is quiet and short-lived. After she is killed, he devotes his life to raising their child. It is the first note of the swan song he so poignantly interpreted almost a decade later in *The Misfits*. But MGM was reportedly shocked at what Wellman had brought back after the costly location work. *Across the Wide Missouri* was mercilessly pared down to seventy-eight minutes and it remains a rambling, episodic film in which

only the vignettes stick in the mind and not one of them revolves around Gable.

After playing himself in one scene of *Callaway Went Thataway,* Gable appeared in *Lone Star* (1952) as a sort of Rhett Butler figure minus the carpetbagging, opportunistic elements. From the onset, he believes in Sam Houston's plans for the annexation of Texas and persuades a latter-day Scarlett (Ava Gardner) to share his ideals and forsake the Wallace Beery type, played by Broderick Crawford.

The Gable character is as dull as Vincent Sherman's direction: he admits that he has been "riding and fighting for ten years," but all of his exploits seem to be safely locked away in the past, like skeletons in closets. Gable's co-star, Broderick Crawford, had won an Academy Award three years before, in 1949, playing a Huey Long type in *All the King's Men.* In *Lone Star,* the contrast between his role and Gable's is significant, because the growing pessimism of American movies was leaving Gable behind as a reformed tough, barely a notch above a reformed drunk in the scales of boredom.

In his last nine years at MGM, Gable's films were often not remakes, but reorientations of his

117

Gable relaxing, 1951

NEVER LET ME GO (1953).On the set

previous movies. *Never Let Me Go* (1953) has Gable as an American news correspondent married to a Russian ballerina (Gene Tierney) and trying to rescue her from commissars. It is really *Comrade X* minus the slapstick, directed with remarkable eclecticism by Delmer Daves, a man who started as an action director in *Destination Tokyo* and moved on to the soppy sentimentality of *Susan Slade* and *A Summer Place. Never Let Me Go* has elements of both styles and is eminently forgettable.

Gable always worked with the best of directors—Capra excepted—in their most tangential films or not at all. He would have been a fine Howard Hawks character but though the two men were friends and hunting companions, they never realized the several projects they discussed. And in *Mogambo* (1953) Gable was given another potentially good director for him, but John Ford made the film brilliantly—and atypically.

Following the revised Gable pattern, *Mogambo* was a soulful remake of *Red Dust*. Ford, the great man of action, gave it the odd elegance of a drawing room comedy in a safari tent. To top reversal with reversal, this legendary director of men handed

118

*LONE STAR (1952). With Ava Gardner*

*NEVER LET ME GO (1953). With Karel Stepanek*

*MOGAMBO (1953). With (left to right) Grace Kelly, Donald Sinden, Eric Pohlmann, Philip Stainton, Ava Gardner*

the picture to Ava Gardner on a silver platter. He covertly shifted the emphasis of the plot to Gardner, allowed her to improvise some of her lines, and put her safely on her way to an Academy Award nomination. She plays the Harlow character with much of the vulgarity toned down and her great scene is a confession to a priest, through venetian blinds, with the rhythm of tom-toms obliterating the words. This sequence points out the difference between *Red Dust* and *Mogambo,* because

Harlow's hip-swinging whore would have been laughable in this sudden attack of jungle repentance. Gable, who merely dallied with Mary Astor in the earlier version, is genuinely smitten with Grace Kelly in the remake.

The Gable character was changed from a plantation manager to a Hemingwayesque white hunter. The screenplay, again credited to John Lee Mahin, endows *Mogambo* with echoes of Hemingway's "The Short Happy Life of Francis Macomber" and

*BETRAYED (1954). With Lana Turner*

Gable's performance suggests how much better he would have been than Gregory Peck as a Hemingway prototype in *The Snows of Kilimanjaro* and *The Macomber Affair*. Gable played the role superbly and his scenes with both Ava Gardner and Grace Kelly proved his sexual aura was still undiminished at fifty-two.

*Betrayed* (1954) was his last film with Lana Turner and also his last one at MGM. In this grim spy movie, Gottfried Reinhardt's dim direction makes the Gable-Turner pair so humorless and sexless that the main attraction is the villain, Victor Mature, who is quite diverting as he almost gives himself a harelip by sneering through the melodramatics.

*Mogambo* had turned out to be a great hit, but by then it was too late for Gable and Metro. The marriage had ended bitterly. The studio did not renew his contract when it expired in 1954, considering he was no longer worth the $520,000 a year he was getting. He left, an angry, dethroned King, less hurt by the years of sad waste of his talent than by the small share he received out of the *Gone with the Wind* bonanza.

Amazed by the box-office strength of *Mogambo*, MGM

had second thoughts and tried to lure him back several times, but to no avail. He would toy with their terms, discuss the idea, and walk out at the last moment. This way he missed a chance to play a role that was perfect for him in Vincente Minnelli's *Home from the Hill*. Robert Mitchum grabbed it and it brought him closer to the niche of substitute Gable he still occupies.

Gable's reluctance to do business with Metro worked both ways, since it also saved him from Minnelli's *The Four Horsemen of the Apocalypse,* a remake originally planned for Marlon Brando, who wisely turned it down. Gable was next in line for refusal and he reportedly laughed uproariously at whoever was crazy or stupid enough to think he could dance a tango à la Rudolph Valentino. Glenn Ford eventually had the misfortune to be involved in that costly fiasco.

Away from MGM and demanding a substantial percentage of the gross, Gable became the highest paid of free-lance actors. His first film on those terms was *Soldier of Fortune* (1955) at 20th Century-Fox. The audience had reacted favorably to the Gable-Kelly chemistry in *Mogambo* and gossip columnists

122

*SOLDIER OF FORTUNE (1955). With Michael Rennie*

were dropping hints of an imminent May-December marriage. He wanted Kelly for *Soldier of Fortune* but she had other commitments. He co-starred with Susan Hayward, who by then had inherited Joan Crawford's penchant for imposing a pseudo-tragic style on cheap melodrama. Hayward seems more comfortable than Gable in *Soldier of Fortune,* possibly because her role is practically identical to the part she played in *Garden of Evil,* a picture she had just then finished with Gary Cooper.

Gable's personal life was going through a bad period. After MGM fired him he had become increasingly withdrawn and moody. Capra had discovered years before that Gable was always better in long takes and full shots, but they had become impossible because he was drinking heavily during this time. He had trouble remembering lines and Edward Dmytryk had to direct *Soldier of Fortune* very carefully, keeping the camera from focusing on Gable's palsied hands. The film was indifferently received.

Finally, in 1955, the tide

*THE TALL MEN (1955). As Ben Allison*

turned right for him, personally and professionally. That year he married Kay Spreckels, who led him back to clean living on the ranch. At Encino, with Kay and her children, he regained the will to live he had lost with Lombard's death. His pride as an actor also needed a boost and he got it—in spades—in his next three films, all directed by Raoul Walsh.

Walsh's directorial style is well within the *macho* code the star exemplified and he approached Gable as a true movie myth, a celluloid Zeus with a thunderbolt in every fist. In *The Tall Men* (1955), the best of their trio of pictures, Gable makes his first appearance with poetic impact: he is silhouetted against snow, emerging from the wild like the last remnant of the outdoor past in American folklore.

As befits an earthly god, Gable's lines in *The Tall Men* are cryptic, oracular. Galloping out of the untamed woods he looks at the dead body of a hanging man and snarls: "We have arrived at civilization." When bad man Robert Ryan tells him that "Luck is against us," he defies augury by replying: "Then we'll try to change it." He is just but not self-righteous, materialistic but not greedy.

Gable only wants enough money to retire to a ranch of his own, but Jane Russell—the Harlow-harlot figure of fifties movies—is discouraged by his lack of ambition and temporarily deserts him, after an erotic and funny tussle under a blanket during a blizzard. Russell's avarice does not infect Gable and he settles for his modest share, leaving Ryan most of the loot. A repentant Russell joins him at fade-out. The audience liked Gable's newest incarnation and *The Tall Men* was one of the most profitable films of 1955.

The second Gable-Walsh collaboration was *The King and Four Queens* (1956), the star's only venture into production with his one-shot company, Gabco. Walsh heavily banked on the Gable sex magic and cast him as a go-getter who tantalizes a quartet of women with assorted tricks of his trade, just to get one of them to reveal the whereabouts of a cache of money.

The film is a fascinating failure because Gable, in his own way, plays very much the same character Chaplin did in *Monsieur Verdoux*. He is a covetous but not murderous Landru and there's a great deal of humor in seeing him court the women, each in a subtly different manner. Its random pleasures and

*THE TALL MEN (1955). On the set*

126

*THE KING AND FOUR QUEENS (1956). With Eleanor Parker*

Gable's multi-layered performance do not save *The King and Four Queens* from seeming diluted and incoherent.

Walsh gave the clue to the film's problems when he was interviewed by *Cahiers du Cinema* in 1964. No matter how they changed the screenplay or fiddled with the editing, Jo Van Fleet as the grizzly bear of a mother-in-law stole the picture from under everyone's nose, including Gable's, who had partly financed it. Trying to wrest the film away from her, Gabco— meaning Gable and company— tore it to shreds. Gable then went through the entire era of actor-producers without ever repeating the experience. In a typical self-deprecatory tone he re-

*BAND OF ANGELS (1957). With Yvonne de Carlo and Patric Knowles*

marked that he'd never learned to be an actor, so he had no business trying to produce or direct.

Walsh soothed Gable's bruised ego with the third and last of their films together. He went further into the deification of his star in *Band of Angels* (1957), loosely based on a novel by Robert Penn Warren. Gable is such an awesome figure that his mere presence at a slave auction sends the competition into shivers. He successfully bids for the octoroon Amantha (Yvonne de Carlo), but only to save her from a degrading future. He takes her to

*RUN SILENT, RUN DEEP (1958). With Burt Lancaster*

his Olympian mansion and proves himself a gentleman by pointedly ignoring her as a sex object. Walsh relied on telluric forces and atmospheric phenomena to bring his Jupiter and Juno together, drenched and sexy, in a flashing thunderstorm.

The Walsh-Gable films were entertaining enough, but the awesome symbolism was getting a little out of hand with *Band of Angels,* so Gable moved on to *Run Silent, Run Deep* (1958), an action-packed submarine *Moby Dick*. He plays a commander whose submarine was sunk by a Japanese Akikaze des-

129

*TEACHER'S PET (1958). With Peter Baldwin and Doris Day*

troyer. The enemy ship becomes his White Whale and it begins to haunt his nightmares. When he gets command of his next submarine, he drills the men with obsessive precision for that inevitable encounter with his prey. He even disobeys orders to stalk his mechanical Moby Dick down the Bongo straits.

Burt Lancaster plays Starbuck to Gable's Ahab. He is resentful and mutinous at first, but is slowly drawn into the frenzy of the pursuit. While Gable is dying, he is ready to carry on. Director Robert Wise's impersonal, clockwork style was just

130

what the material needed and *Run Silent, Run Deep* may not be up to Melville's tale but it is still a good film of its genre.

For Gable, it also functions as a reversal of *Mutiny on the Bounty*. He fumes admirably as a nonsadistic Captain Bligh while John Gay's screenplay allots the Fletcher Christian rebelliousness to Lancaster. Furthermore, Gable has substantially the same role he played in *Command Decision,* but in *Run Silent, Run Deep* his performance is safely anchored in the ethos of the man of action, with no room for paralyzing self-doubts.

Producers William Perlberg and George Seaton then signed Gable for three comedies at Paramount. *Teacher's Pet* (1958) confronts Gable's brashness with Doris Day's primness. He is a self-taught reporter who has risen to city editor and she is a professor of journalism. Gable convinces Day that newspapermen are born and not academically trained, an easy task for the actor since this was his ninth role as a journalist.

The pairing of Hollywood's aging stud with Day, the screen's oldest certified virgin, had infinite potential for sarcasm, but only a fraction of it was realized by director George Seaton, since *Teacher's Pet* was not meant to be a sex comedy. The casting, nonetheless, was inspired and the good lines in the Michael and Fay Kanin screenplay turned it into a pert, reasonably funny, and financially successful film.

Walter Lang, one of Gable's best friends, had for years wanted to do a remake of *Accent on Youth,* a Samson Raphaelson play that had been filmed in the early thirties with Herbert Marshall and Sylvia Sidney. Gable had come to accept his age and he liked playing the theatrical producer who is wooed by a much younger actress (Carroll Baker).

The film was finally titled *But Not for Me* (1959) and under Lang's sophisticated direction Gable gives a sensible and very engaging performance. It is the movie where, in rejecting Carroll Baker's advances, he admits on screen that he is fifty-seven and is getting "too old for this kind of thing." Yet he did not follow this sage advice when he next co-starred with Sophia Loren in *It Started in Naples* (1960).

The film is an embarrassing throwback to his heyday as an irresistible woman tamer. In a climactic scene, Loren starts stripping him coquettishly of his

*BUT NOT FOR ME (1959). As producer Russell Ward*

*BUT NOT FOR ME (1959). With Lee J. Cobb and Lilli Palmer*

tie and jacket while they undulate on a dance floor. He embraces her tightly and the sequence dissolves in a fuzzy, Vaselined close-up of her ecstatic face. The traditional symbolic fade-out indicated Loren had received the Gable treatment: in the next shot she is seen releas-ing a dozen balloons into the dawn-lit skies of Capri.

Gable had put on a lot of weight and in *It Started in Naples* he looked portly, middle-aged, and more than a little annoyed at all the half-hearted sexual innuendo. It is a shame the film ended up so mere-

133

tricious and vapid, for it contained the germ of a fine idea for Gable. He plays a veteran who comes back to Italy fifteen years after the war and sees the country not with the eager eyes of an impressionable soldier but from the jaundiced point of view of a Philadelphia bank manager.

All that was glamorous has now become treacherous, and on potentially hostile ground he counters with his own hostility and growls at waiters who offer him *espresso* or *cappuccino* instead of plain coffee, and at the unreliable ferry operator who changes schedules without bothering to tell anybody. As an unctuous Vittorio De Sica invites him to step into a tiny Italian car, he sneers: "Do we sit on it or do they pack us in olive oil?"

Gable's "ugly American businessman on vacation" is a perfect gem of observation as he goes into mild fits of tourist paranoia, asking everyone: "What kind of a runaround am I getting from all of you?" Reviewing this film, *The New Yorker* said that Gable "often sounds exactly like President Eisenhower." Writers Melville Shavelson and Jack Rose, who had co-authored four screenplays for Bob Hope, gave Gable many an acid quip and also made him sound a lot like Hope.

On this level, *It Started in Naples* could have been a snappy comedy of bad manners, but the plot moved on to a very arch triangle, with Gable and Loren competing for the affection of his brother's child, who is also her nephew. Melville Shavelson must have thought of himself as a good director of children, i.e. *Houseboat* and *The Seven Little Foys*. In *It Started in Naples* he launched an obnoxious brat called Marietto, who single-handedly could have blighted a much better movie than this one.

In Italy, while making *It Started in Naples,* Gable received the screenplay of *The Misfits* (1960). Even for such a poor judge of vehicles, it must have struck a chord, since in so many ways the character of Gaylord Langland is the definitive statement of Gable the actor, the star, the man. Arthur Miller conceived the original story, "The Mustangs," as the saga of misplaced cowboys, left behind by the modern West, who make a miserable living out of chasing wild horses and selling them for dog food.

The screenplay is laden with symbolic overtones as the mustang-chasing begins to stand for the struggle between conformity and self-pride, with Gaylord's

*IT STARTED IN NAPLES (1960). With Sophia Loren*

soul as the battleground. The collateral theme is that it is possible for people to sell their work without selling themselves. Gable, who for twenty-three years was MGM's commodity, must have read between the lines. To underscore the identification, the character's nickname became Gay, also short for Gable.

As a matter of pride, Gable wanted a last, great film. His marriage to Kay Spreckels was happy and he constantly talked about retiring to his ranch. Yet he sometimes told friends that he still had "another good picture" in him. He also com-

*Gable with fifth and last wife Kay  Spreckels*

plained that audiences would remember him mostly for *Gone with the Wind,* a film he never grew to like.

Everyone involved with *The Misfits* was convinced that it would be "the definitive American film," a creature as elusive as the great American novel. Producer Frank Taylor, director John Huston, and writer Miller started chasing the White Whale, and this time Gable was a willing, fervent Starbuck. He trained for the part of Gay as he never had before. He studied nights, trying to find new meanings in the part. And he started the picture in a glow: nobody knew it yet, but his wife was expecting a child, who was to be his only offspring.

*The Misfits* was shot almost totally in chronological sequence, and scene by scene Gable grows on the screen into a new awareness of himself. At first, he is still trying too hard for the fading image and it is saddening to watch him go through all the motions and mannerisms as if he really meant all that empty bravado. Gay, the aging cowboy, is attempting to seduce Roslyn (Marilyn Monroe) with the old oblique grin, one eye almost closed, the other bulging nervously.

He approaches Roslyn with lips pursed as if to suppress a wolf whistle. When she tells him she doesn't feel *that way* about him, he retorts, "Don't get discouraged, girl, you might," in a last desperate stab at the bygone *brio.* Then he becomes increasingly tender, almost avuncular, even wistfully mentioning that she must be a size twelve, like his grown-up daughter.

Their first night in bed gives way to a soothed, delicately shaded morning after. He has prepared breakfast for Roslyn, though he still defensively points out that he won't make a habit of it. They settle into a peaceful relationship, but they both sense that time is running out. Miller's screenplay abounds in stagey perorations but it is the throwaway lines that catch the mood, as when Perce, a young cowboy (Montgomery Clift), drinks to "my old friend Gay" and Roslyn —mistaking the emphasis— rushes gallantly to say, "But Gay's not old."

Gay-Gable's pretensions continue for a while, but then comes a scene of such power and beauty that it ought to shame anyone who ever called Gable a mechanical actor. Gay's teenage children have turned up during a rodeo, accidentally finding him drunk and boisterous in a

*THE MISFITS (1961). As cowboy Gay Langland*

bar. Trying to link the present to the past, he runs back to Roslyn, eager to introduce her to the kids, who are never seen in the film. When he arrives with his girl friend, the son and daughter have fled in embarrassment.

Gay has been lying like the old Gable, fast-talking Roslyn into believing the kids almost knocked him down in their rush to embrace him, because they were so happy to see their father. Finally, here is a dream he can't sell anybody, least of all himself. A cloud of bafflement passes over his features as he realizes the kids were just fidgety and ashamed of him. In a fit of rejected parenthood, Gay goes berserk, runs around drunkenly screaming for his children, and makes a pitiable spectacle.

The scene is a long way from Gable's epic drinking bouts in *Test Pilot* or *Boom Town*. In *The Misfits,* the mad binge is a pathetic closing of old doors and a groping for new ones. When Roslyn is able at last to drag him home, he frenziedly asks her if she would have a child by him and the scene, magnificently played, is reminiscent of Willy Loman insanely planting seed in the middle of the night, near the climax of Miller's *Death of a Salesman.*

Gay knows that he is leaving nothing of his own behind, now that his son and daughter have turned their backs on him. He only has this frail paradise where he and Rosyln can play at being in love. It is soon invaded by an evil influence. Eli Wallach is Guido, the Gable sidekick, rancorous because he lost Roslyn to an older man. He tempts Gay to come back to the *macho* pleasures of chasing wild horses.

In *The Misfits,* every previous element of the Gable screen legend takes on a deeper shade of black, and Wallach plays Guido as if the darker side of the Tracy figure were finally out in the open. The benign Sancho Panza has become a malignant kibitzer who goads his Don Quixote on to increasingly impossible feats.

In the last, powerful half hour of *The Misfits,* Guido-Wallach reveals what Tracy kept hidden in the thirties films he so hated to do. Wallach, a much less genial actor, releases all of Guido's sexual envy at not measuring up to Gay. He feverishly admires the cockeyed courage of Gay and Perce in a rodeo, with the same rapt attention Tracy focused on Gable's exploits. Roslyn becomes hysterical watching the brutal punishment but Guido insists that Gay and Perce do it because it's dangerous, because they might get

*THE MISFITS (1961). With (left to right) Eli Wallach, Thelma Ritter, Marilyn Monroe*

killed. The scene corresponds exactly to the one in *Test Pilot* when Tracy sees flames in Gable's plane and soothes Myrna Loy by shouting "He's asbestos." Yet Wallach's performance is satanic, not angelic.

Gay, Perce, and Guido go mustanging and they bring Roslyn along. She is revolted to see how they frighten, chase, and rope the animals. The rancor at losing Roslyn to Gay makes Guido explode at last in a tirade of antifeminism. Roslyn is the interloper into their world. They are together as men and all women must be shut out. "They're all crazy," Guido shrieks, "They only use you because you need them."

In the light of this scene, it is revealing to find out that one of the hurdles of the screenplay was the character of Guido. Only Tracy had been able to play a Gable sidekick without Freudian implications. *The Misfits* stopped production for two days while Miller was asked to clarify Guido's motives. Director Huston demanded: "I don't care if he turns out to be a homosexual, but he has to be *something!*"

The problem is not difficult to diagnose: Wallach's fine performance had turned the faithful pal into a wily Mephistopheles. He and Roslyn fight for possession of Gay-Gable's soul. When Gay realizes the mustangs are worthless, he whispers to the men: "Let's give them to her. She'll cut them loose," but the girl interrupts by offering him two hundred dollars for the horses. With a withering Gable look of injured pride, he turns on her, saying: "Who do you think you've been talking to all this time?"

Yet the woman has left her mark on him. Seen through her eyes, his life has suddenly become denuded of all its false outdoors glamour. When Roslyn persuades Perce to untie the horses, Gay pursues the stallion, fights savagely with the animal, and subdues it. He has proved himself to be the stronger and so, in a fine moment, he cuts loose the horse he has just roped and offers the animal as a final gift of his manhood to the woman. There is no mistaking the symbolism because Huston even frames it in a crotch shot. It is the one shattering last-reel castration in Gable's career, because this time he really meant it.

It is easy to carp about the faults of *The Misfits*, mainly stemming from the cumbersome Miller screenplay. But Gable believed in it and his belief is as strong as his cynicism used to be. For instance, when Monroe asks him "Do you have a home?" he barely looks around the barren tract of land on both sides of the road before he says: "Right here." The disarming sincerity of his delivery cleanses the calculated pathos of the two-word reply.

In Marilyn Monroe, he found the synthesis of all the leading ladies who besieged him through the years while he was pretending to chase them. As Roslyn, Monroe was a Freudian Harlow, a half-baked tart with spiritual aspirations, part dumb blonde, part misguided child of nature. The role was written *con amore* by Arthur Miller and the performance is at the same time voluptuous and jittery, delightful and annoying, with frequent undertones of Vivien Leigh's Blanche DuBois in Elia Kazan's *A Streetcar Named Desire*. The early Gable would have been crushingly impatient with the likes of Roslyn, but time had given his character a gift of understanding and pity. He put on kid gloves to handle this iron butterfly.

At the end of *The Misfits*,

Gay-Gable is supremely relaxed as he accepts his destiny. He is through with "roping a dream" and knows he must stay with Roslyn because she is the only thing he has to live for. Guido venomously shouts at him, "You'll end up making change in a laundromat," but Gable finds cathartic hope in defeat as he murmurs: "I must find another way to be alive . . . if there's one anymore."

Could there have been another screen life for Gable? It is impossible to say because irony tagged him to the very end. In *The Misfits* he reached new stature as an actor and the film turned out to be his last. On November 4, 1960, Gable said his last words in front of a camera: "Just head for that big star. It will take us home." Four days later he suffered a heart attack; twelve days later he was dead. *The Misfits* is a painful movie to watch, as Gable struggles with the horses, straining his heart to the limit for one more shot, one more performance, one more film.

*The Misfits* is a premonitory, almost spooky film. The cast now reads like an obituary page. Gable, Monroe, Montgomery Clift, Thelma Ritter: they are all gone. Even Paula Strasberg is gone: as Monroe's private acting coach she haunted the production, clad in solid black, like a Stanislavskian specter, preaching the code of sinking your soul into your part.

It was she, unknowingly, who provided the best inverse epitaph for Clark Gable when one day she lamented on the set that "the actor is the only artist who, when he dies, his creation dies with him." She was wrong; Gable the man is dead and buried but his creation has survived him.

He was a King for thirty years and men just don't die when they have made history. William Gable disappeared somewhere between Hopedale and Akron, Ohio. Billy Gable vanished in Oklahoma. Clarke Gabel closed out of town in some touring show, never to be heard from again. But Clark Gable has survived them all.

Somewhere, someplace, right at this very moment, he is there, on a grainy TV image, in the whirring coils of a 16 mm. projector or on that invisible memory screen that is hidden inside every filmgoer's mind. He winks at Harlow, snarls at Garbo, laughs at Crawford. Time and space and death are an illusion compared to his overwhelming reality. Gable is alive and well and living up there on the screen.

142

# BIBLIOGRAPHY

Agee, James. *Agee on Film*. Beacon Press, Boston, 1958.

Baxter, John. *Hollywood in the Thirties*. Paperback Library, New York, 1970.

Bergman, Andrew. *We're in the Money*. New York University Press, New York, 1971.

Capra, Frank. *The Name Above the Title*. The Macmillan Company, New York, 1971.

Carpozi, George, Jr. *Clark Gable*. Pyramid Books, New York, 1961.

Clarens, Carlos. "Gable's Career", *Films in Review*, December, 1961.

Crowther, Bosley. *Hollywood Rajah*. Holt, Rinehart & Winston, New York, 1968.

Davison, Bill. *The Real and the Unreal*. Harper & Brothers, New York, 1962.

Deschner, Donald. *The Films of Spencer Tracy*. Citadel Press, New York, 1968.

Durgnat, Raymond. *Films and Feelings*. M.I.T. Press, Cambridge, 1967.

Essoo, Gabe. *The Films of Clark Gable*. Citadel Press, New York, 1968.

Ferguson, Otis. *Collected Film Criticism*. Temple University Press, Philadelphia. 1971.

Goode, David. *The Story of "The Misfits."* The Bobbs-Merrill Co., Indianapolis. 1963.

Lambert, Gavin, *On Cukor*. G. P. Putnam's Sons, New York, 1972.

MacDonald, Dwight. *On Movies*. Prentice-Hall, Englewood Cliffs, 1969.

Marion, Frances. *Off With Their Heads!* The Macmillan Company, New York, 1972.

Noames, Jean Louis. "Interview with Raoul Walsh." *Cahiers du Cinema*, April 1964.

Nolan, William F. *John Huston: King Rebel.* Sherbourne Press, Los Angeles, 1965.

Reid, John Howard. "The Man Who Made GWTW." *Films and Filming*, December 1967.

Shipman, David. *The Great Movie Stars: The Golden Years.* Crown Publishers, New York, 1970.

Thomas, Bob. *King Cohn.* G. P. Putnam's Sons, New York, 1967.

——*Selznick.* Doubleday & Company, Garden City, New York, 1970.

Tyler, Parker. *The Hollywood Hallucination.* Simon & Schuster, New York, 1970.

Warner, Jack. *My First Hundred Years in Hollywood.* Random House, New York, 1964.

Zierold, Norman. *The Moguls.* Coward-McCann, New York, 1969.

# THE FILMS OF CLARK GABLE

The director's name follows the release date. A (c) following the release date indicates that the film was in color. Sp indicates Screenplay and b/o indicates based/on.

1. THE PAINTED DESERT. Pathé, 1931. *Howard Higgin.* Sp: Tom Buckingham & Howard Higgin. Cast: William Boyd, Helen Twelvetrees, William Farnum. Western with CG as cowboy.

2. THE EASIEST WAY. MGM, 1931. *Jack Conway.* Sp: Edith Ellis, b/o play by Eugene Walter. Cast: Constance Bennett, Adolphe Menjou, Robert Montgomery, Anita Page, Marjorie Rambeau, Clara Blandick. Rich man's mistress is ruined. CG had small role as her brother-in-law.

3. DANCE, FOOLS, DANCE. MGM, 1931. *Harry Beaumont.* Sp: Richard Schayer, b/o story by Aurania Rouverol. Cast: Joan Crawford, Lester Vail, Cliff Edwards, Natalie Moorhead. Girl wins confidence of gang to learn who killed reporter. CG was gang chieftain.

4. THE FINGER POINTS. First National, 1931. *John Francis Dillon.* Sp: John Monk Saunders, b/o story by Saunders & W. R. Burnett. Cast: Richard Barthelmess, Fay Wray, Regis Toomey, Robert Elliott. Reporter turns crooked for underworld. CG played gang leader.

5. THE SECRET SIX. MGM, 1931. *George Hill.* Sp: Frances Marion, b/o her story. Cast: Wallace Beery, Jean Harlow, Lewis Stone, John Mack Brown, Ralph Bellamy. CG as reporter who cracks crime ring.

6. A FREE SOUL. MGM, 1931. *Clarence Brown.* Sp: John Meehan, b/o book by Adela Rogers St. Johns. Cast: Norma Shearer,

Lionel Barrymore, Leslie Howard, James Gleason. Rich man's daughter falls for gangster (CG). Remade as *The Girl Who Had Everything* (1953).

7. LAUGHING SINNERS. MGM, 1931. *Harry Beaumont.* Sp: Bess Meredyth, b/o play *Torch Song* by Kenyon Nicholson. Cast: Joan Crawford, Neil Hamilton, Marjorie Rambeau, Guy Kibbee, Cliff Edwards, Roscoe Karns. Salvation Army Worker (CG) helps troubled entertainer.

8. NIGHT NURSE. Warners, 1931. *William A. Wellman.* Sp: Oliver H. P. Garrett, b/o novel by Dora Macy. Cast: Barbara Stanwyck, Joan Blondell, Ben Lyon, Charlotte Merriam, Charles Winninger. Nurse helps mistreated children. CG as villainous chauffeur.

9. SPORTING BLOOD. MGM, 1931. *Charles Brabin.* Sp: Willard Mack & Wanda Tuchock, b/o novel *Horseflesh* by Frederick Hazlitt Brennan. Cast: Madge Evans, Ernest Torrence, Lew Cody, Marie Prevost. Racing melodrama, with CG as owner of gambling place.

10. SUSAN LENOX—HER FALL AND RISE. MGM, 1931. *Robert Z. Leonard.* Sp: Wanda Tuchock, b/o novel by David Graham Phillips. Cast: Greta Garbo, Jean Hersholt, John Miljan, Alan Hale. Ruined girl finally finds salvation with engineer (CG).

11. POSSESSED. MGM, 1931. *Clarence Brown.* Sp: Lenore Coffee, b/o play *The Mirage* by Edgar Selwyn. Cast: Joan Crawford, Wallace Ford, Skeets Gallagher, Frank Conroy. CG as politically ambitious lawyer with romantic problems.

12. HELL DIVERS. MGM, 1931. *George Hill.* Sp: Harvey Gates and Malcolm Stuart Boylan, b/o story by Lt. Commander Frank Wead. Cast: Wallace Beery, Conrad Nagel, Dorothy Jordan, Marjorie Rambeau. CG as battling officer in Naval Air Force.

13. POLLY OF THE CIRCUS. MGM, 1932. *Alfred Santell.* Sp: Carey Wilson, b/o play by Margaret Mayo. Cast: Marion Davies, C. Aubrey Smith, Raymond Hatton. Reverend (CG) marries circus performer.

14. STRANGE INTERLUDE. MGM, 1932. *Robert Z. Leonard.* Sp: Bess Meredyth & C. Gardner Sullivan, b/o play by Eugene O'Neill. Cast: Norma Shearer, Robert Young, Alexander Kirkland, Ralph Morgan, May Robson. Film version of O'Neill's marathon play, with CG as heroine's doctor lover.

15. RED DUST. MGM, 1932. *Victor Fleming.* Sp: John Lee Mahin, b/o play by Wilson Collison. Cast: Jean Harlow, Mary Astor, Gene Raymond, Donald Crisp. Plantation owner in Indonesia (CG) finds romance and trouble. Remade as *Mogambo* (1953).

16. NO MAN OF HER OWN. Paramount, 1932. *Wesley Ruggles.* Sp: Maurine Watkins & Milton H. Gropper, b/o story by Edmund Goulding & Benjamin Glazer. Cast: Carole Lombard, Dorothy Mackaill, Grant Mitchell, George Barbier, Elizabeth Patterson. Girl becomes involved with gambler (CG).

17. THE WHITE SISTER. MGM, 1933. *Victor Fleming.* Sp: Donald Ogden Stewart, b/o novel by F. Marion Crawford and Walter Hackett. Cast: Helen Hayes, Lewis Stone, Louise Closser Hale, Edward Arnold, May Robson. Girl becomes nun after believing that her lover (CG) has died in the war. Third film version of story.

18. HOLD YOUR MAN. MGM, 1933. *Sam Wood.* Sp: Anita Loos & Howard Emmett Rogers, b/o story by Anita Loos. Cast: Jean Harlow, Stuart Erwin, Dorothy Burgess, Muriel Kirkland. Girl falls for heel (CG) who reforms after she lands in prison.

19. NIGHT FLIGHT, MGM, 1933. *Clarence Brown.* Sp: Oliver H. P. Garrett, b/o novel by Antoine de Saint-Exupery. Cast: Helen Hayes, John Barrymore, Lionel Barrymore, Myrna Loy, Robert Montgomery, William Gargan. Aviation drama with CG as pilot.

20. DANCING LADY. MGM, 1933. *Robert Z. Leonard.* Sp: Allen Rivkin & P. J. Wolfson, b/o novel by James Warner Bellah. Cast: Joan Crawford, Franchot Tone, May Robson, Winnie Lightner, Robert Benchley, Fred Astaire, Nelson Eddy. Musical about a dancer and a theatrical producer (CG).

21. IT HAPPENED ONE NIGHT. Columbia, 1934. *Frank Capra.* Sp: Robert Riskin, b/o story "Night Bus" by Samuel Hopkins Adams. Cast: Claudette Çolbert, Walter Connolly, Roscoe Karns. Fleeing heiress encounters reporter (CG). Gable won Academy Award. Remade as *You Can't Run Away From It* (1956).

22. MANHATTAN MELODRAMA. MGM, 1934. *W. S. Van Dyke.* Sp: Oliver H. P. Garrett & Joseph L. Mankiewicz, b/o story by Arthur Caesar. Cast: Myrna Loy, William Powell, Leo Carrillo, Nat Pendleton. Two boys grow up to go opposite ways. CG played the wicked one who goes to the chair.

23. MEN IN WHITE. MGM, 1934. *Richard Boleslavski.* Sp: Waldemar Young, b/o play by Sidney Kingsley. Cast: Myrna Loy, Jean Hersholt, Elizabeth Allen, Otto Kruger, Wallace Ford. CG as dedicated doctor who must decide between love and duty.

24. CHAINED. MGM, 1934. *Clarence Brown.* Sp: John Lee Mahin, b/o story by Edgar Selwyn. Cast: Joan Crawford, Otto Kruger, Stuart Erwin, Una O'Connor, Akim Tamiroff. Girl marries rich man but loves another (CG).

25. FORSAKING ALL OTHERS. MGM, 1934. *W. S. Van Dyke.* Sp: Joseph L. Mankiewicz, b/o play by Edward Barry Roberts & Frank Morgan Cavett. Cast: Joan Crawford, Robert Montgomery, Charles Butterworth, Billie Burke, Rosalind Russell, Arthur Treacher. Comedy with CG as one-third of romantic triangle.

26. AFTER OFFICE HOURS. MGM, 1935. *Robert Z. Leonard.* Sp: Herman J. Mankiewicz, b/o story by Laurence Stallings & Dale Van Every. Cast: Constance Bennett, Stuart Erwin, Billie Burke, Harvey Stephens. Newspaper editor (CG) and society girl get involved in murder.

27. CHINA SEAS. MGM, 1935. *Tay Garnett.* Sp: Jules Furthman & James Keven McGuiness, b/o novel by Crosbie Garstin. Cast: Jean Harlow, Wallace Beery, Rosalind Russell, Lewis Stone, Robert Benchley, C. Aubrey Smith. Ship's captain (CG) gets mixed up with blonde and Malaysian pirates.

28. CALL OF THE WILD. Twentieth Century, 1935. *William Wellman.* Sp: Gene Fowler & Leonard Praskins, b/o novel by

Jack London. Cast: Loretta Young, Jack Oakie, Frank Conroy, Reginald Owen. Film version of classic novel, with CG as miner Jack Thornton.

29. MUTINY ON THE BOUNTY. MGM, 1935. *Frank Lloyd.* Sp: Talbot Jennings, Jules Furthman, and Carey Wilson, b/o novel by Charles Nordhoff & James Norman Hall. Cast: Charles Laughton, Franchot Tone, Herbert Mundin, Dudley Digges, Donald Crisp, Movita. As Fletcher Christian, CG leads mutiny against villainous Captain Bligh. Remade in 1962 with Marlon Brando in CG role.

30. WIFE VS. SECRETARY. MGM, 1936. *Clarence Brown.* Sp: Norman Krasna, Alice Duer Miller & John Lee Mahin, b/o story by Faith Baldwin. Cast: Myrna Loy, Jean Harlow, May Robson, James Stewart. CG's secretary arouses his wife's jealous instincts.

31. SAN FRANCISCO. MGM, 1936. *W. S. Van Dyke.* Sp: Anita Loos, b/o story by Robert Hopkins. Cast: Jeanette MacDonald, Spencer Tracy, Jack Holt, Jessie Ralph, Shirley Ross, Ted Healy. Barbary Coast cabaret owner romances singer. With famous climactic sequence of San Francisco earthquake of 1906.

32. CAIN AND MABEL. Warners, 1936. *Lloyd Bacon.* Sp: Laird Doyle, b/o story by H. C. Witwer. Cast: Marion Davies, Allen Jenkins, Ruth Donnelly, Roscoe Karns, Walter Catlett. Romance of prizefighter (CG) and musical comedy star.

33. LOVE ON THE RUN. MGM, 1936. *W. S. Van Dyke.* Sp: John Lee Mahin, Manuel Seff & Gladys Hurlbut, b/o story by Alan Green and Julian Breen. Cast: Joan Crawford, Franchot Tone, Reginald Owen, Donald Meek, Mona Barrie. Rival foreign correspondents vie for heiress. CG wins.

34. PARNELL. MGM, 1937. *John M. Stahl.* Sp: John Van Druten & S. N. Behrman, b/o play by Elsie T. Schauffler. Cast: Myrna Loy, Edna May Oliver, Edmund Gwenn, Donald Crisp, Billie Burke, Alan Marshal. CG as controversial Irish leader.

35. SARATOGA. MGM, 1937. *Jack Conway.* Sp: Anita Loos & Robert Hopkins. Cast: Jean Harlow, Lionel Barrymore, Walter Pidgeon, Frank Morgan, Una Merkel. Bookmaker (CG) meets

granddaughter of old breeder of throughbreds.

36. TEST PILOT. MGM, 1938. *Victor Fleming.* Sp: Vincent Lawrence & Waldemar Young, b/o story by Lt. Commander Frank Wead. Cast: Myrna Loy, Spencer Tracy, Lionel Barrymore, Samuel S. Hinds, Marjorie Main. Dashing test pilot (CG) has problems on the ground and aloft.

37. TOO HOT TO HANDLE. MGM, 1938. *Jack Conway.* Sp: Laurence Stallings & John Lee Mahin, b/o story by Len Hammond. Cast: Myrna Loy, Walter Pidgeon, Walter Connolly, Leo Carrillo. Adventures of a newsreel cameraman (CG).

38. IDIOT'S DELIGHT. MGM, 1939. *Clarence Brown.* Sp: Robert E. Sherwood, b/o his play. Cast: Norma Shearer, Edward Arnold, Joseph Schildkraut, Burgess Meredith, Laura Hope Crews. Song-and-dance man (CG) and fake countess meet on the eve of a world war.

39. GONE WITH THE WIND. MGM, 1939. *Victor Fleming.* Sp: Sidney Howard, b/o novel by Margaret Mitchell. Cast: Vivien Leigh, Leslie Howard, Olivia de Havilland, Hattie McDaniel, Thomas Mitchell, Butterfly McQueen, Evelyn Keyes, Ann Rutherford. CG in his most famous role as Rhett Butler in drama of old South.

40. STRANGE CARGO. MGM, 1940. *Frank Borzage.* Sp: Lawrence Hazard, b/o novel *Not Too Narrow, Not Too Deep* by Richard Sale. Cast: Joan Crawford, Ian Hunter, Peter Lorre, Paul Lukas, Albert Dekker. Group of men escape from tropical prison, led by CG.

41. BOOM TOWN. MGM, 1940. *Jack Conway.* Sp: John Lee Mahin, b/o story "A Lady Comes to Burkburnett" by James Edward Grant. Cast: Spencer Tracy, Claudette Colbert, Hedy Lamarr, Frank Morgan, Lionel Atwill, Chill Wills. "Wildcatters" have trouble with oil and women. CG wins Colbert.

42. COMRADE X. MGM, 1940. *King Vidor.* Sp: Ben Hecht & Charles Lederer, b/o story by Walter Reisch. Cast: Hedy Lamarr, Oscar Homolka, Felix Bressart, Eve Arden. Romance of newspaperman (CG) and Russian streetcar conductor.

43. THEY MET IN BOMBAY. MGM, 1941. *Clarence Brown.* Sp: Edwin Justus Mayer, Anita Loos & Leon Gordon, b/o story by John Kafka. Cast: Rosalind Russell, Peter Lorre, Jessie Ralph, Reginald Owen. Confidence man (CG) and jewel thief fall in love, get involved in war.

44. HONKY TONK. MGM, 1941. *Jack Conway.* Sp: Marguerite Roberts & John Sanford. Cast: Lana Turner, Frank Morgan, Claire Trevor, Marjorie Main, Albert Dekker, Chill Wills. Western with CG as gambling hall sharpster.

45. SOMEWHERE I'LL FIND YOU. MGM, 1942. *Wesley Ruggles.* Sp: Marguerite Roberts, b/o adaptation by Walter Reisch of story by Charles Hoffman. Cast: Lana Turner, Robert Sterling, Patricia Dane, Charles Dingle. Reginald Owen. CG as newspaperman involved in love and adventure in World War II.

46. ADVENTURE. MGM, 1945. *Victor Fleming.* Sp: Frederick Hazlitt Brennan & Vincent Lawrence, b/o novel *This Strange Adventure* by Clyde Brion Davis. Cast: Greer Garson, Thomas Mitchell, Joan Blondell, Tom Tully, John Qualen, Richard Haydn. Sailor (CG) meets and marries librarian.

47. THE HUCKSTERS. MGM, 1947. *Jack Conway.* Sp: Luther Davis, b/o adaptation by Edward Chodorov & George Wells of novel by Frederick Wakeman. Cast: Deborah Kerr, Ava Gardner, Edward Arnold, Sydney Greenstreet, Adolphe Menjou, Keenan Wynn. Business and amatory tribulations of advertising man (CG).

48. HOMECOMING. MGM, 1948. *Mervyn LeRoy.* Sp: Paul Osborn, b/o adaptation by Jan Lustig of story by Sidney Kingsley. Cast: Lana Turner, Anne Baxter, John Hodiak, Ray Collins, Gladys Cooper, Cameron Mitchell. Doctor (CG) learns about life and love from a nurse in wartime.

49. COMMAND DECISION. MGM, 1948. *Sam Wood.* Sp: William R. Laidlaw & George Froeschel, b/o play by William Wister Haines. Cast: Walter Pidgeon, Van Johnson, Brian Donlevy, Charles Bickford, John Hodiak, Edward Arnold. Air Force general (CG) faces life-and-death decisions.

50. ANY NUMBER CAN PLAY. MGM, 1949. *Mervyn LeRoy.* Sp: Richard Brooks, b/o novel by Edward Harris Heth. Cast: Alexis Smith, Wendell Corey, Audrey Totter, Frank Morgan, Mary Astor, Barry Sullivan, Lewis Stone, Leon Ames, Marjorie Rambeau. CG as owner of gambling casino with personal problems.

51. KEY TO THE CITY. MGM, 1950. *George Sidney.* Sp: Robert Riley Crutcher, b/o story by Albert Reich. Cast: Loretta Young, Frank Morgan, Marilyn Maxwell, Raymond Burr, James Gleason, Lewis Stone. Mayor (CG) meets lady mayor at convention.

52. TO PLEASE A LADY. MGM, 1950. *Clarence Brown.* Sp: Barre Lyndon & Marge Decker. Cast: Barbara Stanwyck, Adolphe Menjou, Will Geer, Roland Winters. Auto racer (CG) tangles with columnist.

53. ACROSS THE WIDE MISSOURI. MGM, 1951. *William A. Wellman.* Sp: Talbot Jennings, b/o story by Jennings & Frank Cavett, suggested by book by Bernard De Voto. Cast: Ricardo Montalban, John Hodiak, Adolphe Menjou, Jack Holt, Maria Elena Marques. Frontiersmen invade Indian country in 1829. CG as their leader.

54. LONE STAR. MGM, 1952. *Vincent Sherman.* Sp: Borden Chase & Howard Estabrook, b/o story by Chase. Cast: Ava Gardner, Broderick Crawford, Lionel Barrymore, Beulah Bondi, Ed Begley, Moroni Olsen. Western with CG as adventurer-cattleman.

55. NEVER LET ME GO. MGM, 1953. *Delmer Daves.* Sp: Ronald Millar & George Froeschel, b/o novel *Come the Dawn* by Roger Bax. Cast: Gene Tierney, Bernard Miles, Richard Haydn, Belita, Kenneth More, Karel Stepanek, Theodore Bikel. Newspaperman (CG) rescues his ballerina-wife from behind the Iron Curtain.

56. MOGAMBO. MGM, 1953. (c) *John Ford.* Sp: John Lee Mahin, b/o play by Wilson Collison. Cast: Ava Gardner, Grace Kelly, Donald Sinden, Philip Stainton, Eric Pohlmann. Adventure and romance in Africa with big-game hunter (CG). Remake

of *Red Dust* (1932).

57. BETRAYED. MGM, 1954. (c) *Gottfried Reinhardt.* Sp: Ronald Millar & George Froeschel. Cast: Lana Turner, Victor Mature, Louis Calhern, O. E. Hasse, Wilfrid Hyde-White. CG as Dutch intelligence man in World War II.

58. SOLDIER OF FORTUNE. 20th Century-Fox, 1955. (c) *Edward Dmytryk.* Sp: Ernest K. Gann, b/o his novel. Cast: Susan Hayward, Michael Rennie, Gene Barry, Tom Tully. Kingpin operator in Hong Kong (CG) rescues photographer from Communist China.

59. THE TALL MEN. 20th Century-Fox, 1955. (c) *Raoul Walsh.* Sp: Sydney Boehm & Frank Nugent, b/o novel by Clay Fisher. Cast: Jane Russell, Robert Ryan, Cameron Mitchell. Western with CG leading cattle drive to Montana.

60. THE KING AND FOUR QUEENS. United Artists, 1956. (c) *Raoul Walsh.* Sp: Margaret Fitts & Richard Alan Simmons, b/o story by Miss Fitts, Eleanor Parker, Jo Van Fleet, Barbara Nichols. Con-man (CG) works to get money away from widow and her four daughters-in-law.

61. BAND OF ANGELS. Warners, 1957. (c) *Raoul Walsh.* Sp: John Twist, Ivan Goff & Ben Roberts, b/o novel by Robert Penn Warren. Cast: Yvonne de Carlo, Sidney Poitier, Efrem Zimbalist Jr., Patric Knowles, Rex Reason. CG as wealthy man in antebellum South.

62. TEACHER'S PET. Paramount, 1958. (c) *George Seaton.* Sp: Fay & Michael Kanin. Cast: Doris Day, Gig Young, Mamie Van Doren, Nick Adams. Romance of newspaper editor (CG) and journalism teacher.

63. RUN SILENT, RUN DEEP. United Artists, 1958. *Robert Wise.* Sp: John Gay, b/o novel by Commander Edward L. Beach. Cast: Burt Lancaster, Jack Warden, Brad Dexter, Don Rickles. Submarine drama with CG as commander.

64. BUT NOT FOR ME. Paramount, 1959. *Walter Lang.* Sp: John Michael Hayes, b/o play *Accent on Youth* by Samson Raphaelson. Cast: Carroll Baker, Lilli Palmer, Lee J. Cobb, Barry

Coe, Thomas Gomez. Broadway producer (CG) has problem with a doting secretary.

65. IT STARTED IN NAPLES. Paramount, 1960. (c) *Melville Shavelson*. Sp: Melville Shavelson, b/o story by Michael Pertwee & Jack Davies. Cast: Sophia Loren, Vittorio De Sica, Marietto. Man (CG) clashes with Italian girl over custody of his dead brother's son.

66. THE MISFITS. United Artists, 1961. *John Huston*. Sp: Arthur Miller. Cast: Marilyn Monroe, Montgomery Clift, Eli Wallach, Thelma Ritter, James Barton, Estelle Winwood. CG in his last role as aging cowboy.

# INDEX

*(Page numbers italicized indicate photographs)*

157

158

## ABOUT THE AUTHOR

René Jordan has written extensively on films for many publications, including *Film Quarterly, The Village Voice, Films in Review, Cinema,* and *Film Ideal.* He lives in New York City.


## ABOUT THE EDITOR

Ted Sennett has been attending and enjoying movies since the age of two. He has written about films for magazines and newspapers, and is the author of *Warner Brothers Presents,* a survey of the great Warners films of the thirties and forties. A publishing executive, he lives in New Jersey with his wife and three children.